JACK'S MANUAL

On the VINTAGE and PRODUCTION, CARE
and HANDLING of WINES, LIQUORS, ETC.

By J. A. GROHUSKO

A HANDBOOK OF INFORMATION
FOR HOME, CLUB
OR HOTEL

RECIPES FOR FANCY MIXED
DRINKS AND WHEN AND
HOW TO SERVE

THIRD EDITION

PUBLISHED BY

J. A. GROHUSKO, :: 60 STONE ST., NEW YORK

COPYRIGHTED BY
JACOB A. GROHUSKO
NEW YORK

Classic Cocktail Guides
and Retro Bartender Books

Jack's Manual of Recipes for Fancy Mixed Drinks and How to Serve Them

A Pre-Prohibition Cocktail Book

J. A. Grohusko

Historic Cookbooks of the World
Kalevala Books, Chicago

"Always do sober what you said you'd do drunk. That will teach you to keep your mouth shut." — Ernest Hemingway, 1899–1961

Jack's Manual of Recipes for Fancy Mixed Drinks and How to Serve Them:
A Pre-Prohibition Cocktail Book

© 2010 Compass Rose Technologies, Inc. All rights reserved. No part of this book may be reproduced in any manner whatsoever without written permission, except in the case of brief quotations embodied in critical articles and reviews. Originally published as *Jack's Manual on the Vintage and Production, Care and Handling of Wines, Liquors, Etc.: A Handbook of Information for Home, Club, or Hotel. Recipes for Fancy Mixed Drinks and When and How to Serve* by J. A. Grohusko, © 1910, third edition. Title page illustration courtesy of Dover Publications, Inc., New York.

ISBN: 978-1-880954-28-7

Joanne Asala, Editor
Historic Cookbooks of the World

Rowan Grier, Series Editor
Classic Cocktail Guides
and Retro Bartender Books

Classic Cocktail Guides and Retro Bartender Books and *Historic Cookbooks of the World* are published by Kalevala Books, an imprint of Compass Rose Technologies, Inc., PO Box 409095, Chicago, IL 60640. Titles published by Kalevala Books are available at special quantity discounts to use as premiums and sales promotions or for academic use. For more information, please write to the Director of Special Sales, Compass Rose Technologies, Inc., PO Box 409095, Chicago, IL 60640 or contact us through our Web site, www.CompassRose.com.

Editors' Note

Some ingredients found in vintage cocktail guides are unavailable or hard to come by today. Check out our resource guide at the back for vendors who specialize in hard-to-find ingredients and websites with information on how to recreate classic cocktails and cocktail ingredients.

INDEX

A

	Page
Absinthe	26
Absinthe Cocktail	26
Absinthe Dripped	26
Absinthe Frappe	26
Ale Beanie Cocktail	26
Alexander Cocktail	27
An Ale Cup	27
Ale Sangaree	27
Amer Picon Highball	27
Anderson Cocktail	27
Angostura Fizz	27
Angostura Ginger Ale	28
Angostura Grape-fruit	28
Appollinaris Lemonade	28
Applejack Coctail	28
Applejack Sour	28
Apple Toddy	28
Ardsley Cooler	28
Arf & Arf	29
Astringent	29
Auditorium Cooler	29
Aviator	29

B

Bacardi Cocktail	29
Bachelor's Rose	29
Baltimore Egg Nogg	29
Ballor Cocktail	30
Bambo Cocktail	30
Baraccas Cocktail	30
Barry Cocktail	30
Bath Cocktail	30
B. B. Highball	30
Beals Cocktail	30
Beef Tea	31
Benz Cocktail	31
Bicarbonate of Soda	31
Big Four	31
Bijou Cocktail	31
Billin Cocktail	31
Bishop	31
Bismarck Cocktail	32
Black Hawk Cocktail	32
Blackthorne Cocktail	32
Black Stripe	32
Bogerz Coctail	32
Bonnett Cocktail	33
Bornn's Cocktail	33
Boston Cooler	33
Bottle of Cocktails	33
Bowl of Egg Nogg	33
Brandy burned with Peach	33
Brandy Champrelle	34
Brandy Cocktail	34
Brandy Crusta	34
Brandy Daisy	34
Brandy Fix	34

	Page
Brandy Fizz	34
Brandy Flip	35
Brnady Float	35
Brandy & Ginger Ale	35
Brandy High-Ball	35
Brandy Julep	35
Brandy Punch	35
Brandy Rickey	35
Brandy Sangarce	36
Brandy Scaffa	36
Brandy Smash	36
Brandy & Soda	36
Brandy Sour	36
Brandy Toddy	36
Bronx Cocktail	36
Bronx Terrace	37
Brooklyn Cocktail	37
Brut Cocktail	37
Bud's Cocktail	37
Butcher Cocktail	37
Byrrh Cocktail	37
Byrrh Wine Daisy	38
Byrrh Wine Rickey	38

C

Cafe Folies Bergere	38
Calisaya Cocktail	38
California Sherry Cobbler	38
Campill Cocktail	38
Canadian Fizz	38
Captain Cocktail	39
Catawba Cobbler	39
Champagne Cobbler	39
Champagne Cocktail	39
Champagne Cup	39
Champagne Frappe	39
Champagne Julep	39
Champagne Punch	40
Champagne Sour	40
Champagne Velvet	40
Chocolate Cocktail	40
Chocolate Punch	40
Cris Cocktail	40
Christie Cocktail	41
Cider Cup	41
Cincinnati Cocktail	41
Clarendon Cocktail	41
Claret Cobbler	41
Claret Cup	41
Claret Lemonade	42
Claret Punch	42
Cleaves Delight	42
Cliftin Cocktail	42
Clover Club Cocktail	42
Cocktail a la Furey	42
Clover Leaf	43
Coffee Cocktail	43
Coffee Kirsch	43

Historic Cookbooks of the World

	Page
Cognac a la Russe	43
Columbus Cocktail	43
Coney Cocktail	44
Consolidated Cocktail	44
Cook Cocktail	44
Coronation Cocktail	44
Cotton Cocktail	44
Creme de Menthe on Ice	44
Creme de Menthe Highball	44
Cuban Cocktail	44
Curacao Punch	45
Cushman Cocktail	45

D

	Page
Daniel Webster Punch	45
Dean Cocktail	45
Devil's Cocktail	45
Dog Days	45
Donnelly's	45
Dorr Cocktail	46
Dry Martini Cocktail	46
Dubonnet Cocktail	46
Dunham Cooler	46
Duplex Cocktail	46

E

	Page
Edner Cocktail	46
Egg Lemonade	46
Egg Nogg, Plain	47
Egg Phosphate	47
Egg Sour	47
Elk's Delight	47
Evans Cocktail	47
Evans Cooler	47
Evans Shandy Gaff	48

F

	Page
Fairbanks Cocktail	48
Fancy Brandy, Gin and Whiskey Cocktails	48
Fancy Claire	48
Fancy Whiskey Mash	48
Farmers' Cocktail	48
Fedora Cocktail	49
Fine Lemonade for Parties	49
Fish House Punch	49
Folies Bergere Cocktail	49
Folies Bergere Cooler	49
Folies Bergere Pousse Cafe	49
Fowler Cocktail	49
Frank Hill Cocktail	50
Freeman's Bliss	50
French Flag	50

G

	Page
Gin Bump	50
Gin and Calamus	50
Gin and Milk	50
Gin Cocktail	50
Gin Crusta	51
Gin Daisy	51
Gin Fizz	51
Gin Fix	51
Gin Highball	51
Gin Julep	51
Gin and Molasses	51
Gin Punch	52
Gin Rickey	52
Gin Sangaree	52
Gin Smash	52
Gin Sour	52
Gin and Tansy	52
Gin Toddy	53
Glasgow Fizz	53
Good Luck Night Cap	53
Gould's Rickey	53
Graham Cocktail	53
Grenadine Highball	53
Guggenheimer Cocktail	54
Gum Syrup	54

H

	Page
Half and Half	54
Hamersley Cocktail	54
Harvard Cocktail	54
Hamilton Cocktail	54
Hock Cobbler	54
Holstein Cocktail	55
Honolulu Cocktail	55
Horses Neck	55
Hot Brandy Sling	55
Hot Egg Nogg	55
Hot Gin Sling	55
Hot Irish Punch	55
Hot Lemonade	56
Hot Milk Punch	56
Hot Rum	56
Hot Scotch	56
Hot Scotch Toddy	56
Hot Scotch Whiskey Sling	56
Hot Spiced Rum	56
Hudson Coctail	57
Hunter Cocktail	57

I

	Page
Ideal Cocktail	57
Illinois Thunderbolt	57
Imperial Egg Nogg	57
Improved Manhattan Cocktail	57
Improved Martini Cocktail	57
Irving Cocktail	58
Isabelle Cocktail	58
Italian Cocktail	58
Italian Wine Lemonade	58

J

	Page
Jack Kaiser Favorite	58
Jack Rabbit Cocktail	58
Jack Rose	58
Jamaica Rum Sour	59
Japanese Cocktail	59
Jack Zeller Cocktail	59
Jenks Cocktail	59
Jersey Cocktail	59
Jersey Lily Pousse Cafe	59
Jersey Sour	59
Jersey Sunset	60
John Collins	60
Judge Smith Cocktail	60
Junkins Cocktail	60
June Daisy	60
June Rose	60

Classic Cocktail Guides and Retro Bartender Books

K

	Page
Kirschwasser Punch	61
Knickebein	61
Knickerhocker	61
Knickerbocker Baked	61

L

Larchmont Cocktail	61
La Roche Cocktail	61
Lawrence Cocktail	61
Lemonade	62
Leonora Cocktail	62
Leowi Cocktail	62
Liberal Cocktail	62
Little Maxine	62
Lone Tree Cocktail	62

M

Magnus	63
Maiden's Dream	63
Mamie Taylor	63
Manhattan Cocktail	63
Mary Garden Cocktail	63
Marguerite Cocktail	63
Martini Cocktail	63
May Wine Punch	64
Medford Rum Punch	64
Medford Rum Smash	64
Medford Rum Sour	64
Merry Widow	64
Metropolitan Cocktail	65
Milk Punch	65
Milk Shake	65
Milk & Seltzer	65
Mill Lane Cocktail	65
Millionaire's Cocktail	65
Mint Julep	65
Mississippi Punch	66
Montana Club Cocktail	66
Montgomery	66
Morning Cocktail	66
Morning Glory Fizz	66
Morning Glory	67
Morton's Favorite	67
Moselle Cup	67
Mulled Ale	67
Mulled Ale or A Burton-on-Trent	67
Mulled Claret	68
Murphy Cocktail	68

N

National Guard Punch	68
New Orleans Fizz	68
Nicholas Cocktail	68
North-Pole Cocktail	68

O

Old Delaware Fishing Punch	69
Old Fashioned Cocktails	69
Olivette Cocktail	69
Ojen Cocktail	69
Old Oxford College Mulled Ale	69
"One Yard of Flannel" or "Ale Flip"	70
Opal Cocktail	70
Orange Cocktail	70
Orangeade	70
Orchard Punch	70
Orgeat Punch	70
Oxford University "Nightcap"	71
Oyster Bay Cocktail	71
Oyster Cocktail	71

P

Palmer Cocktail	71
Palmetto Cocktail	71
Parisian	71
Parisian Pousse Cafe	72
Parson's Cocktail	72
Pat Cocktail	72
Patrick Cocktail	72
Peach and Honey	72
Perfect Cocktail	72
Pheasant Cocktail	72
Philadelphia Bronx	72
Phoebe Delights	73
Picon Cocktail	73
Plain Lemonade	73
Pope Highball	74
Porter Cocktail	74
Port Wine Cobbler	74
Port Wine Flip	74
Port Wine Punch	74
Port Wine Sangaree	74
Postmaster	74
Pousse Cafe	75
Pousse L'Amour	75
Preparing Rock and Rye	75
Punch a la Romaine	75

Q

Queen's Highball	75

R

Randolph	76
Raphael Cocktail	76
Raymond Cocktail	76
Red Lion Cocktail	76
Regent Punch	76
Remsen Cooler	76
Renaud's Pousse Cafe	77
Rhine Wine Cobbler	77
Rhine Wine and Seltzer	77
Rhine Wine Cup	77
Richmond Cocktail	77
Robert Burns	77
Rob Roy Cocktail	77
Robinson Cocktail	78
Rocky Mountain Cooler	78
Rogers Rock	78
Roman Punch	78
Rossington Cocktail	78
Royal Smile	78
Royal Smile Cocktail	78
Royal Fizz	79
Royal Punch	79
Ruby Cocktail	79
Rum Daisy	79
Rum Flip	79
Rye Highball	80
Rye Whiskey Rickey	80

S

	Page
Sabbath Morning Calm	80
Sam Ward	80
Sankey Punch	80
Saratoga Cocktail	80
Sauterne Cobbler	80
Sauterne Cup	81
Scheuer Cocktail	81
Schulke Cocktail	81
Scotch Highball	81
Seltzer Lemonade	81
Scotch Whiskey Rickey	81
Shandy Gaff	81
Sherry and Angostura	82
Sherry and Bitters	82
Sherry Cobbler	82
Sherry Cocktail	82
Sherry and Egg	82
Sherry Flip	82
Sherry Wine Punch	82
Sherry Wine Sangaree	82
Shonnard Cocktail	83
Silver Cocktail	83
Silver Fizz	83
Silverman	83
Sirloin	83
Sloe Gin Bump	83
Sloe Gin Cocktail	83
Sloe Gin Fizz	84
Sloe Gin Highball	84
Sloe Gin Rickey	84
Soda Cocktail	84
Soda Lemonade	84
Soda Negus	84
Soul Kiss	85
Starboard Light	85
Stanton Cocktail	85
Star Cocktail	85
St. Charles Punch	85
St. Croix Crusta	85
St. Croix Fizz	86
St. Croix Rum Punch	86
St. Croix Sour	86
Stone Fence	86
Stonewall	86
Story Cocktail	86
Stony Lonesome	86
Swan Cocktail	86
Swiss Ess	87

T

	Page
Terminal Cooler	87
Tip Top Punch	87
Tom and Jerry	87
Tom Collins Brandy	88
Tom Collins Gin	88
Tom Collins Rum	88
Tom Collins Whiskey	88
Treasurer Cocktail	88

	Page
Trilby Cocktail	88
Trowbridge Cocktail	88
Tucker Cocktail	88
Turf Cocktail	89
Turf Club Cocktail	89
Turkish Sherbet	89
Turn Cocktail	89
Tuxedo Cocktail	89

V

Van Lee Cocktail	90
Vanilla Punch	90
Van Zandt Cocktail	90
Velvet Champagne	90
Vermouth Cocktail	90
Vermouth Frappe	90
Vermouth Highball	90
Vichy	90
Virgin Cocktail	91

W

Washington Cocktail	91
Watkins Cocktail	91
Write Horse	91
White Lion	91
White Plush	91
White Rat	92
Whiskey Cobbler	92
Whiskey Cocktail	92
Whiskey Crusta	92
Whiskey Daisy	92
Whiskey Julep	92
Whiskey Fix	92
Whiskey Fizz	93
Whiskey Flip	93
Whiskey Float	93
Whiskey Punch	93
Whiskey Rickey	93
Whiskey Sling	93
Whiskey Smash	93
Whiskey Sour	94
Whiskey Toddy	94
Widow's Dream	94
Widow's Kiss	94
Williams Cocktail	94

Y

York Cocktail	94

Z

Zabriskie	94
Zaza Cocktail	95
Zazarack Cocktail	95

———o———

Delicacies ....95 to 97

INTRODUCTORY

The author, in presenting this volume to the public, begs to state that his intention in compiling it is not to have it recorded as one of the literary marvels of the day, but to give to the "prince of good fellows" a guide of value for his home, club, hotel or café.

As previously stated in his first issue, it is only practical experience, through long association with the leading American hotels and clubs, which enables him to publish this volume, the most complete of its kind ever issued.

In the various recipes, reference is made only to wines and ingredients of the highest character.

In the advertising section, contained at the end of this book, the reader will find only such products as have been preferred by the author; and as their use has proven satisfactory and pleased many thousand guests, he would suggest their preference in your mixing.

That the reader may be familiar with the various sizes and the terms used in this publication, the following table will prove of value, but only applies to liquor, *i. e.*, whiskey, gin, etc., other ingredients additional:

1 Jigger	= ½	whiskey glass.
100%	= ½	" "
50%	= ¼	" "
25%	= ⅛	" "

half whiskey glass being regarded as a full portion for one person.

If you, my friend, at any time wish advice relating to the subject of mixed drinks or beverages, and will correspond with the author, your communication will receive prompt and careful attention.

In closing, one request is made of the reader: If through the pages of this work you find its contents of value, suggest it to your friends, that we all may drink to each other's health.

THE AUTHOR.

PRODUCTION OF CHAMPAGNE

Champagne is produced in the Department of Marne, where grapes were cultivated as far back as the sixth century. In the last will and testament of Remy, Archbishop of Rheims, dated A. D. 530, he bequeathes to the clergy of his diocese, vineyards situated in the neighborhood of that city. The growth of the Champagne district has continually increased since the tenth century, and viticulture has become a very important industry. The real development of champagne dates from the eighteenth century, when Dom Perignon, a monk of the Abbey of Hautvillers, near Epernay, discovered the method of making sparkling champagne. The Champagne district seems to have a special influence over the fruit grown upon it, for the grapes possess a perfume and other qualities not found in grapes grown anywhere else. The soil is composed of chalk with a light covering of earth, which gives the grapes their distinctive qualities, producing a sparkling wine which cannot be equalled. Many people think that champagne is made from a white grape, but not more than one-quarter of the grapes grown in the Champagne vineyards are white, the rest being black. Great precaution is taken not to crush the grapes when gathering, the bunches being detached from the vine one by one, and carefully sorted according to their ripeness, and in some locations every individual grape is examined. The grapes are pressed daily in a large press, worked by hand, and the must (juice) is separated at once from the stalk and skin, which contains the coloring matter. This liquid is almost colorless, and after fermentation becomes still lighter in color. The juice obtained from the press by three consecutive pressings, gives the cuvée, and it is this liquid which has the necessary qualities to make a fine wine. The wines obtained by subsequent pressure are called **vins de suite,** and are inferior in quality, and cannot be used for choice champagne.

As the must runs out of the press, it is put into vats, where it is left to settle for twelve hours to allow impurities to settle at the bottom. It is then drawn off into casks, the cleanliness of which is scrupulously looked after. A few days later fermentation commences and changes the sweet liquid into an alcoholic one, which is wine. When cold weather sets in, the wine becomes clear and is drawn off, the lees remaining in the cask.

The wine-producing district of Champagne may be divided into three regions. First, the mountain country of Rheims, where the grapes possess the distinctive qualities of vinosity and freshness; second, the Avize district, notable for wines made from white grapes, which are of great delicacy; and third, the Valley of the Marne, where the wines are characterized by an excellent bouquet. Wines made solely from grapes of any one district would be found disappointing. One must unite the freshness and strength of Verzenay with the mellowness of Bouzy, the softness of Cramant, and the bouquet of Ay, in order to blend into a champagne all the delightful qualities which a connoisseur expects to find. During January and February the winemaker mixes in immense casks the wines from different vineyards. Wines want character, bouquet, vinosity and delicacy, and these qualities can only be secured by the mixture of wines possessing these elements individually. To make a fine champagne one must know thoroughly the characteristics of the wine of each vineyard, and this requires a keen sense of smell and taste, and great skill and experience.

THE CUVÉE.

During the spring the merchant makes the "Cuvée," which is the assembling of a number of wines in one blend; depending upon the business of the merchant it may be a few or many thousand bottles and until finally disposed of is known as the "Special Cuvée" of the year of blending. "Vintage years" are the years of especially fine crops and in such years the Cuvée is made as large as proper qualities permit. The making of the Cuvée is the most delicate operation in the profession, requiring exquisite judgment in the selection of the wines to be blended to produce the perfect Cuvée, a definite result being obtained only after a period of years as the wine rounds out in maturity in the bottle.

BOTTLING

By the aid of mechanical apparatus the wine, to which is added a certain quantity of cane sugar, is put into new and carefully rinsed out bottles; these are corked and the cork held in by means of an iron clasp. The bottles are immediately stored on their sides in immense cellars, hewn from solid chalk.

SERVING

The process of uncorking this wine is often grossly mismanaged. The cork should be slowly and noiselessly extracted after, first the wire, and then the string, are entirely removed. The glass must be near at hand so that no wine may be lost. Care should be taken that the wine flows out quietly, and if gently poured on the side of the wine glass the ebullition of the wine will be checked and the goblet filled without spilling. Do not fill the glass to the brim with any wine, but leave a quarter of an inch or more free. Rich champagne only requires to be stood in ice up to the shoulder of the bottle for not longer than twenty minutes, even in the hottest weather. It is important to remember that too much icing destroys body and vinosity. Served with ice puddings a rich champagne is delicious, or even after soup, but it would be considered cruel to provide nothing but champagne during the whole of a dinner. Should champagne be required between luncheon and dinner, it is well to serve a biscuit with it.

AMERICAN CHAMPAGNES.

Wines made in America—There are many excellent types which resemble the better foreign qualities in many essentials. They are clean and palatable, with a good deal of "mousse." They are good "Dinner Wines."

On account of there being no tax or duty on Domestic Champagnes they are much lower in price than the imported.

American Sparkling Wines are produced principally in three territories, viz.:

In **New York State**, in the **Ohio and Missouri District** and in **California**.

New York State produces nearly four-fifths of the output from grapes grown on the steep hills around Hammondsport and Lake Keuka. These wines are light and delicate, resembling much the French Saumurs.

The Ohio and Missouri wines, whilst being heavier in body, are somewhat rougher in flavor.

California, while the largest producer of still wines, has up to the present time, furnished but little champagne.

Great progress has been made for the past few years by Urbana Wine Company wines. They are presenting a red, sparkling Burgundy on the market; making great progress.

FORMING THE SPARKLE

The ferments which existed at the time of the vintage and had become dormant during the winter, revive with the first warmth of spring, and commence to act afresh. They decompose the natural sugar still remaining from the vintage and transform it, as also the cane sugar added at the time of bottling, into a supplementary amount of alcohol and carbonic acid gas; but this time the gas cannot escape because the bottle is hermetically sealed; instead, it mixes thoroughly with the wine, producing that elegant sparkle so well known. This fermentation in the corked bottle generates a deposit which settles on the lower side of the bottle and must be got rid of. This is effected by two operations. These are the "mise sur pointe" and the "disgorgement."

THE MISE SUR POINTE

The bottles are placed head downward through an inclined plank pierced with holes at an angle of 70 degrees. Every day for at least three months a cellarman, specially trained for this kind of work, shakes the bottles lightly against the plank with a wrist movement quick and sharp. The deposit slowly descends and collects on the cork.

"VINTAGES."

The most appreciated vintage wines now in the market are 1898 (a very limited quantity available), 1900 and 1904. The vintage of 1906 is not yet generally marketed, but it will be much appreciated. At the moment, for any event, the discriminator can make no error in the selection of "Brut 1900" or "Brut 1904," for, while the Cuvée of these years was not large, the wine is exquisite in its maturity.

True champagne is naturally effervescent—the sparkle and brilliancy due to a naturally generated carbonic acid gas. Still wines may be charged with gas, imitating champagne, but the result is never satisfactory. It is this method which

RACKS

has been responsible for the delimitation of the district from which wines may be shipped as "Champagne," the French Government permitting the use of the word Champagne only on wine produced naturally in the Department of the Marne. Wine of the Department of Aube may be labelled "Champagne of the Second Zone."

The total area now under cultivation to produce true Champagne, under prescribed regulation is only about 37,000 acres. Contrary to the general understanding Champagne is produced principally from black grapes.

THE DISGORGEMENT

The deposit, having settled on the cork, is now ready to be extracted. To do this the bottle is first placed head downward, to a depth of three inches, in a refrigerating bath. Under the action of the cold, the deposit congeals in the neck of the bottle. The cellarman then takes the bottle out of the bath, holds it upright, undoes the clasp and eases the cork, which the pressure of the carbonic gas inside eventually forces out with a loud report, together with the deposit. The wine is then absolutely clear.

THE LIQUEURING

After disgorging, the wine has not the least taste of sugar, the sugar added at bottling having been completely transformed into alcohol and carbonic acid. Whilst in this state the wine is known as "brut." To regulate it to the client's taste, which varies in different countries, a certain quantity of liqueur, composed of sugar candy and wine from the finest Champagne vineyards, is added immediately after the disgorging.

THE CORKING

For corking, the best Spanish corks are used and are held in by either string and wire or wire muzzle, according to the custom of each house. Finally the capsule and label are put on and the bottles are packed in cases or baskets ready for shipment.

The cellars are located at Rheims, Epernay, Ay, Avize, etc., and are well worth seeing.

ALWAYS A LUXURY

True champagne can never be other than a luxury, from the cost of cultivation, the care in making, the long period elapsing before the wine has reached maturity and principally because of the limited area in which it can be produced. The loss from leakage and breakage is enormous, owing to the pressure upon the bottle, and difficulty of transportation.

SAUTERNES

Un Rayon de Soleil Concentre Dans un Verre (Biarnez).

The region which produces the celebrated white wines universally known under the name of sauternes is situated on the left bank of the Garonne, about 35 kilometers south of Bordeaux, and includes the communes or parishes of Barsac, Bommes, Fargues, Sauternes and Preignac, and a part of Saint-Pierre de Mons.

The country is hilly, admirably exposed to the rays of the sun, which explains, to a great extent, the degree of maturity the grapes attain.

The soil is more or less sandy, argillo-sillico-calcareous in some parts, argillo calcareous (as at Barsac) or entirely argillaceous in others.

There is no doubt that to this particularly favorable soil is due in a great measure the superiority of the Sauterne wines, which it is impossible to equal anywhere else, however careful the vinification may be. But it is only just to add that the selection of the vine plants, the extraordinary care bestowed on the culture of the vineyards, the special and expensive vinification, contribute to ensure perfection in bouquet, color, and finesse in a wine to which no other can be compared, for the simple reason that, of its kind, there exists nothing like it.

The appearance of the vineyards in this region differs from that of the Médoc, inasmuch as the vines are high; the surrounding country in which culture is more varied, is hilly and picturesque, the views from some of the heights, that, amongst others, on which Chateau Yquem is situated, extending miles over fertile scenery.

It would take too much space to describe minutely the labor involved in cultivating these vineyards; each season, or, more exactly, each day, brings its task, and nothing must be neglected, however futile this may appear to the uninitiated.

As before mentioned, the grapes are gathered and pressed in a manner peculiar to the district.

The gathering takes place later than in the Médoc and lasts much longer, commencing at the end of September, and terminating in the first half of November. The grapes are allowed to attain the extreme degree of ripeness, and, after taking a deep golden color, they finally, under the influence of the mycoderma "Botrytis Cinera," become over-ripe, a state absolutely necessary to ensure the quality of the future wine. The berry subsequently becomes browned and roasted, the skin gets thin and cracks, and a sugary juice oozes from it. Little by little, each berry advances to this state until the whole bunch forms, so to speak, but one mass of juicy fruit. It may easily be imagined how fragile the grapes are when they get to this degree of maturity, and how, whilst they gain if the weather remains fine, they are likely to suffer if it becomes rainy.

The gathering is effected in small quantities at a time, and only as each bunch of grapes attains the advanced state described above. Sometimes, and especially in the first growths, each berry is gathered separately and more or less quickly, according to the weather. When rainy, the operations are suspended and resumed when it becomes dry again.

It is easy to see that quantity here is sacrificed to quality, and that the expenses of wine making, under such circumstances, must necessarily be high. It often requires as many as six successive pickings to gather one bunch. The cost of cultivating vineyards in the Sauternes district is estimated to range from 1000 to 1200 francs per hectare, inclusive of grape-picking and purchase of casks; the yield per hectare may be roughly estimated at from 4 to 7 hogsheads, according to the vintage. Vintaged by ordinary methods, the wines would yield about one-third more.

In the superior growths, there are three selections or "tries." The first, comprising the berries which have dried somewhat after becoming over-ripe, yields what is known as "vin de tête." The second selection comprises the berries in a somewhat less advanced state and yields a larger quantity; the third includes the remainder of the grapes, which, although ripe, have not attained the same degree of maturity as the others; the wine pressed from it is called "vin de queue" and is relatively unimportant in quantity.

The grapes are pressed rapidly, so as to prevent the wine from taking too deep a color from the skin. The must

CHATEAU YQUEM

which flows from the press is at once put into casks, where the fermentation takes place almost immediately and lasts several weeks, the duration depending on the style of the wine and on the temperature.

The quality is approximately judged by the musts, but it is only after the first racking, generally when the winter is over, that a definite opinion can be formed. Four rackings a year are necessary, sometimes five for wines of the first picking, and a daily inspection, tasting and filling of the casks, are requisite to ensure proper treatment.

The classed growths are sold under their name, Chateau Yquem being the first and probably the best known. But simply as sauterne, Barsac, bommes, preignac, etc., wines of the highest grade are sold and fetch high prices, the greatest care being bestowed on the small vineyards as on the large ones.

Sauternes—of succeeded vintages—are delicate in flavor, of a pale golden color, mellow, rich, bordering on sweetness, and have a fine, agreeable bouquet; they are hygienic, not heady, and merit the description of perfection in white wines.

Dr. Mauriac, of Bordeaux, says in one of his works: "The great Sauternes white wines, which are of a relatively high alcoholic strength, are both tonic and stimulating; consumed moderately, they are invaluable to convalescents after a severe illness or when it is necessary to revive an organism attenuated by high fever, hemorrhage, or long fatigue.

They are perfect as dessert wines and one or two glasses at the end of a meal facilitate digestion and provoke gaiety.

BURGUNDIES

The wines produced in the Province of Burgundy, situated in eastern France, viz., in the Côte d'Or, between Macon, Beaune and Dijon, rank among the best burgundies. They contain more tartrates and tannin than clarets, and are altogether heavier in body and aroma.

The best known cheaper qualities are Macon, Beaune and Beaujolais, and their names indicate generally the district of their growth. The better wines are Romanee, Canti, Pommard, Chambertin, Nuits and Clos De Vougot, and the best known white wines are the Chablis.

The red burgundies are recommended as blood-making wines, especially in cases of general or local anaemia.

This ancient province, one of the largest and finest of France, embraced before the revolution of 1789 territory which has since formed the Ain, Côte d'Or, Saône et Loire and part of the Yonne departments.

The Dukes of Burgundy were powerful and played an important part in French history; by marriage they had become masters of most of the Dutch provinces. The wealthy Netherland cities contributed to the embellishment of those of Burgundy and the influence of Dutch art is to be detected in many of the architectural beauties of the province.

On the other hand, the inhabitants of Burgundy introduced their wines into Holland and it may be said that from that time their great reputation outside France dates. Even nowadays Belgium and Holland are amongst the most fervent admirers and largest consumers of Burgundies.

Taken as a wine growing country Burgundy extends along the railway line from Sens to Villefranche and includes Beaujolais which, although part of the Rhône Department, produces wines of the same character, and not at all like those of the Lyonnais district to which it belongs administratively and geographically.

Classic Cocktail Guides and Retro Bartender Books

From a viticultural standpoint, it may be divided into three principal districts, the Yonne in the North, Saône et Loire and Rhône in the South, Côte d'Or in the Centre.

Yonne. Known as lower Burgundy produces red and white wines in the administrative divisions of Tonnerre, Auxerre, Avallon and Joigny. In the two first the best growths are located amongst which **Chablis** is the best known.

Saône et Loire comprises two distinct districts, the Mâconnais and the Châlonnais, each of which can be subdivided into several classes or zones producing wines of different character, style and quality.

Rhône. The wines of this department, which are classed with those of Burgundy, are produced in the well known district of Beaujolais, in the administrative arrondissement of Villefranche. The district is divided by a chain of mountains into two parts Upper Beaujolais, in which the best growths are located, and Lower Beaujolais growing more ordinary wines.

Côte d'Or. This beautiful department, which forms Upper Burgundy, possesses the most celebrated growths. The vineyards are situated on the sunny slopes of a chain of mountains running from northeast to southwest, and are most favorably exposed. Unlike the Bordeaux vineyards, they are in general small, varying in size from 4 to 15 hectares.

The vineyards can be classed in three groups:

1. Côte de Beaune in which are located amongst others such growths as Chassagne, Gravieres, Clos Tavannes, Montrachet, Charmes, Goutte d'Or, Santenot, Volnay, Pommard, Beaune, Aloxe, Corton, etc.

2. Côte de Nuits including many of the finest growths, amongst others les Corvées, les Thoreys, les Malconsorts, la Tâche, Romanée-Conti, Richebourg, Clos Vougeot, les Musigny, Chambolle, Clos de Tart, les Lambreys, Chambertin, Clos de Bèze, Clos St. Jacques, etc.

3. Côte de Dijon the least important and which produces in general wines of secondary quality.

As mentioned above, the vineyards are in general small and a great number of them are divided into lots of unequal area; a typical example is the celebrated "Clos de Vougeot" which, although not very extensive, belongs to fifteen proprietors.

The City of Beaune hospitals possess several vineyards, and it is their custom every year, a few days after the gathering, to offer their wines for sale by public auction. The prices realized are always high and, although they are not exactly taken as a basis, it is only after the sale has taken place that the market value of the vintage is judged.

In Burgundy, the vines are cultivated with great care according to tradition dating several centuries back. Very few changes have been made in this long course of years, in fact, the growers are adverse to the adoption of modern methods of culture as recommended by agricultural committees and experts.

The grapes are picked at the end of September or beginning of October according to their degree of ripeness. The fermentation is followed very carefully and the **cuveries** where the wine is made are commodiously built so as to ensure perfect conditions of temperature and cleanliness.

The wines drawn into casks are treated methodically; in February or March following the gathering, they are separated from the lees which are pretty considerable; a second racking takes place in July.

The following year, the wines are racked twice, and normal treatment is continued by fining and racking until they are ready for bottling which is also effected with the utmost care, every precaution being taken to ensure proper development and long preservation. Burgundies are generally bottled when two or three years old.

The characteristics of Burgundy wines are a bouquet and flavor which are inimitable, fine taste, body, sève, all of which qualities constitute one of the finest products under the sun. Each growth or district has naturally its peculiar qualities and varies in value from the ordinary to the highest grades.

Beaujolais are comparatively light, bouqueted and develop rapidly in bottle, Mâcon are firmer with color, are of good preservation, and develop a fair bouquet with age. The Côte d'Or produces a great variety of fine wines, some relatively medium bodied, others very full bodied, rich and fruity.

Burgundy should be served, and is best appreciated, with heavy roasts and large game. At the temperature of the room all its fine qualities develop.

It is estimated that viticultural Burgundy covers a surface of about 45,000 square kilometres, with a population of about one and a half millions.

The vineyards with an area of 83,346 hectares belong to 83,173 owners making an average of one hectare for each.

The average annual production for the decennial period 1897-1906 was:

Yonne	488,500	hectolitres
Saône et Loire	1,401,500	"
Côte d'Or	872,500	"

The figures of the 1907, 1908 and 1909 crops were:

	1907	1908	1909	
Yonne	559,900	427,800	250,800	hectolitres
Saône et Loire	1,204,800	2,306,500	1,015,000	
Côte d'Or	679,200	929,300	404,100	

In 1910 the crop was practically nil and the figures are not worth mentioning.

HOW TO SERVE BURGUNDY

Red Burgundies should be served at the dining-room temperature, having been brought from the cellar several hours before the meal, after having decanted them off their sediment, or by using special baskets in which the bottles are laid just as they lay in the bin.

Burgundy wines in bottle form a sediment, owing to maturing, which is more or less abundant according to the growths and ages. This sediment does not impair the quality of the wine, provided the bottle is uncorked carefully and not shaken so as to disturb the sediment.

The cork having been drawn, the wine should be carefully decanted while holding the bottle up against the light in the same position as it was when stored in the cellar. As soon as the sediment is nearing the neck of the bottle the decanting must be stopped for the mixing of the sediment with the wine will deprive the latter of its bouquet and render it bitter. Bottles should never be left uncorked, for the better the quality of the wine the more apt it is to become flat.

White wines should be left in the cellar until needed.

Sparkling wines should be iced.

CLARETS

The word "claret" means a wine of clear, red color. It is the English name given to the red wines of France, and particularly those grown in the Bordeaux district.

Chateau wines are those made from grapes of a selected character and grown on vineyards of wealthy gentlemen, who devote much time and money in their careful cultivation, storing and aging. Chateau bottled wines rank very high in the estimation of the connoisseur.

Wines described as bearing the Cachet du Chateau are simply those which have the crest or coat of arms bearing that name on the label. The caps and corks are likewise branded.

There are hundreds of districts where good wines are grown. To enumerate their varieties would fill volumes, and with a limited space at disposal it is impossible to give more than superficial indication of the best known brands. The wines of France have a recognized classification, according to value.

Clarets do not throw a deposit as quickly as Port wine, but the greatest care must be exercised in decanting them in order that they may be served in brilliant condition; the sediment being extremely fine, with a bitter flavor, it is not easily detected and will entirely spoil the delicacy of the wine if mixed with it.

Clarets moved from one cellar to another, are temporarily put out of condition; it is like transplanting a tree without giving it time to recover and develop in its new soil, therefore, wine always requires to settle down before being consumed.

Old wines particularly need a rest after a journey, and they should always be taken from the cellar direct to the Dining Room. This is important, but it is a very general omission in hotels and clubs.

Claret, to acquire the proper temperature, should be stood up in the Dining Room the morning it is to be consumed, and decanted at least half an hour before serving. A full wine may be kept a little longer, as it improves by contact with the air. Young or cheap Clarets should also be carefully decanted because any sediment coming into the glass destroys the character of the wine.

It is most inadvisable to serve Claret in a decanting basket, it should always be decanted, because the last one or two glasses invariably run muddy. Claret should, if possible, be put on the table at about the temperature of the room in which it will be consumed, to preserve the delicate freshness of the wine. The bouquet escapes when the wine is exposed to sudden heat or warmed to excess; this bouquet is mainly due to volatile vinous ethers which it is most desirable to retain. Clarets of medium quality improve with age, whereas the lightest table wines may be drunk fresh bottled, as is the custom in France; a fine, large, thin and white glass being used, and only two-thirds filled.

Sherry and stronger wines are liable to throw a deposit in bottle if kept for any length of time; care should therefore be exercised in decanting them or in fact any wine in which a sediment may be formed.

The sound and natural wines of Bordeaux are refreshing and appetizing, and are the best type of a universal beverage for every day use; no other wines which the world produces are capable of yielding such lasting pleasures to the palate. They have also the additional advantage that when mixed with water do not spoil.

When taken with food they entice the languid palate and are admirably adapted for persons of all ages and conditions, whose occupations tax the brain more than the muscles, and as they contain only a comparatively small percentage of alcohol have but little tendency to inebriate.

The dietetic value of Claret has not been over-rated. If taken with food it is of service to persons of the gouty temperament, as it stimulates digestion and does not create acidity. The combination of the various saline ingredients with fruit acids, notably the acid tartrate of potash (Cream of Tartar) make for its highest value.

The delicate aroma and delicious flavor of the finer sorts of after-dinner Claret give endless delight and satisfaction; and there are so many varieties (differing according to the vineyards from which they emanate) they afford the connoisseur a wide scope for the exercise of judgment in selection.

WINES OF ITALY

Italy ranks second in the wine production of the world. Its Brolio is one of the best Italian red wines; it resembles Burgundy, but is somewhat drier on the palate. When old it is a highly tonic wine. Barbera is another good wine; it ranks as good table or dinner wine. Also white Corvo

Capri, Lacrymae Christi are strong, sweet wines of southern Italy. There are many others, both still and sparkling, amongst which may be named Moscato Spumante (sparkling Moselle flavor). Nebiolo Spumante Valpolicella (sparkling) red wine. There is also sparkling Lacrymae Christi.

Italian wines are well known and highly appreciated all over the world.

WINES OF GERMANY

German wines are grown principally on the banks of the Rhine, and are generally known as Hocks. Those grown on the banks of the Moselle are designated as Moselles. There are many varieties of German wines, and their names denote principally the district of their growth.

German wines are of great medical value. They are strengthening to the action of the heart and diffuse cheerfulness, without leaving adverse results, which more alcoholic beverages might produce. Moselle wines especially are prescribed by the medical profession as highly beneficial in all affections of the liver and kidneys. They are considered anti-diabetic in their action and to minimize gouty tendencies.

MOSELLE

Moselle as a highly etheral wine is also very useful in cases of cerebral and cardiac exhaustion, it stimulates the action of the liver and kidneys, and is generally credited with being otherwise beneficial. It is said to be anti-diabetic, and does not increase the gouty tendency.

HOCKS

Hocks have great fragrance and vinosity and are preeminently the wines most suitable for intellectual enjoyment, as they are particularly exhilarating and increase the appetite. Being of light alcoholic strength but rich in volatile ethers, they are exceedingly efficacious, and do not (like Clarets) so quickly spoil after opening.

The finer qualities widely differ in flavor from each other, and being rich in ethers are much valued as a stimulant in sustaining the nervous force of the heart, while its enfeebled muscular tissue has time in which to recuperate.

For serious nervous prostration their value as a remedy can hardly be overestimated; their beneficial effects being strikingly exhibited in bringing back a stronger and steadier heartbeat, thus calming any attendant irritability which is of the utmost importance to the patient.

SWEET BITTERWINES

French wines have been divided into four distinct classes, namely: Red Wines, White Wines, Sparkling Wines and Liqueur Wines. In the latter class are included all the various aperitifs such as Dubonnet, which is an appetizer made from a sweet French wine, strongly infused with a solution of Peruvian bark. Its tonic properties are extensively acknowledged.

Byrrh wine is a high-class appetizing and tonic wine prepared with exceptionally generous wines.

Amer Picon, a French bitters, or aperitif, made from French sweet wine infused from bitter herbs.

Edouard Dubonnet & Labussière is a high-class appetizing and tonic wine, and an exceedingly good stimulant. It is made from old wine infused with bitter herbs and quinquinas. With mineral waters it makes a very refreshing drink.

Absinthe is a highly aromatic liqueur of an opaline, greenish color, and slightly bitter taste. It is distilled from bitter herbs, and is considered tonic and stomachic, although its excessive use produces a morbid, stupefying condition differing from ordinary form of alcoholism. The mode of drinking it is by mixing with water, which is poured into it drop by drop.

SHERRY

There are no wines which can compare with genuine Sherry, either in generous character, delicacy of flavor or dietetic value. It represents about the highest development of quality in wine, is distinguished by freedom from acidity, sugar extractive matter, and has a high proportion of volatile ethers. These compound vinous ethers (to which Wine of a certain class and age owes the greater part of its flavor and bouquet) have a scarcely less important influence in advancing the quality of wine than in providing a valuable stimulant to the vital functions in cases of cerebral and cardiac exhaustion.

It relieves that condition of sleeplessness consequent upon slow and inefficient digestion, of old age. It is also beneficial in the later stages of severe febrile diseases, with great exhaustion and sleeplessness. A really good and pure Sherry has the same effect in rapidly restoring strength and regularity to the heart's action in certain forms of chronic neuroses—also in those severe neuralgic affections which so seriously affect the system.

The older bottled wines and those having the greatest amount of ethers are most effective. The finest wine that can be procured for money is just that which will give the best effect with the least possible delay. It must not be forgotten that the influence of such wine is entirely distinct from that of mere alcohol.

In Spain, where its qualities are well known, it is regularly used by physicians as a restorative in cases of collapse after surgical operations.

It should also be mentioned that it is invaluable for use as medicine (but not as a beverage) in the wasting diseases of children, particularly when they lose weight rapidly. It is conspicuously useful in such cases when the development of tuberculosis is feared.

In opposition to a very general idea, it is the opinion of Dr. Garrott, confidently confirmed by Dr. Francis E. Anstie, in his interesting book, "Uses of Wines in Health and Disease," that the non-saccharine or dry Sherries are not productive of gout, provided they do not cause any disturbance of the digestive functions. Dr. Anstie claims that it is only the saccharine of alcoholic liquors which develop gouty manifestations or evoke the tendency of latent gout.

PORT WINE

In the selection of the Port wine, much depends upon the weather, as the physical conditions of those who partake of it must be considered; people accustomed to open air exercise enjoy generous wines, and in warm weather, light tawny wine should be preferred.

In some houses it is customary to drink a vintage Port no younger than twenty years in bottle, but there are many good wines which mature in from four to six years and acquire sufficient perfection to satisfy the connoisseur who is not too fastidious. If more than one quality of Port wine is required, it is better to commerce with the richer or younger wine and follow with the drier or older.

Port is a valuable medicine, and old crusted Wine a rare luxury.

It represents nearly all the elements of a fine wine, besides being most agreeable to a refined palate. An old bottled wine when judiciously used, with its fine volatile ethers, is singularly useful in restoring strength and regularity to the heart's action, and for certain forms of anemia it is nearly always beneficial. A full flavored potent wine of moderate age retaining much of the richness of its original flavor is for such purposes the best agent, the object being to employ only such wine as will exert the maximum of good influence upon both appetite and digestion.

In case of acute hemorrhage even an excessive quantity of Port Wine administered at the right moment has been found to have the result of resurrection from almost certain death.

LIQUEURS

Benedictine is a high-class liqueur, distilled exclusively at Fecamp, Normandy. It was originally made by the Benedictine monks, but since the French revolution it has been manufactured by a secular company, according to the original recipe. Its medicinal properties are of an acknowledged high order.

Maraschino is made from cherries griottes, grown chiefly in the south of France. It has a unique perfume and an agreeable taste.

Anisette. The basis of this cordial is anis seed. Its properties for facilitating digestion and preventing secondary fermentation, which causes dyspepsia, are well known and acknowledged; it is not only an agreeable but also a salutary cordial, known throughout the world.

Chartreuse is a highly esteemed tonic cordial, obtained by the distillation of various aromatic plants and some species of nettles growing on the Alps. There are some other ingredients and herbs used, but these are a secret belonging to the Carthusian monks, from which order the name Chartreuse is derived. It was formerly distilled by the monks at the monastery of the Grande Chartreuse in France, but since their expulsion it has been made at Tarragona, Spain, where the order is now established.

Sloe Gin is a species of the wild damson. It is a distillation of unsweetened gin, mixed with an infusion of the juice of the sloe berries, and is a delightful cordial. Its medicinal attributes are very special, being slightly laxative and very soothing in cases of griping pain. With hot or cold water it makes a very agreeable drink, and is also used in cocktails, fizzes, rickies, daisies, etc.

Kummel. The foundation of kummel is caraway seed, and its dietetic properties are somewhat similar to anisette. It is invaluable for indigestion or dyspepsia. It is also known in Russia as Alish, and is used there extensively as an after-dinner cordial.

Kirchwasser is a spirituous liqueur obtained by the distillation of Switzerland wild cherries. It is distilled chiefly in Vosges and in the Black Forest. It is free from sweetness, has a delicious flavor of bitter almonds, and is colorless as water.

Crême de Cacao is made from the beans of cacao. The chuao, the finest of which come from Puerto Cabello, is remarkable for its delicacy and perfume, and adds the most delicate effect to the small quantity of alcohol which this cordial contains.

BITTERS

Specifically, they are liqueurs (mostly spirituous) in which herbs, generally bitter herbs, are steeped or infused. Bitters are appetizers and beneficial for other medicinal purposes.

Angostura is a bitter tonic much used in the West Indies as a preventive against malarial fever. It is also used as a flavoring substance for all kinds of drinks, cocktails, etc., to which it imparts a unique flavor. It was originally made at Angostura, a city in Venezuela. Now it is made at Trinidad by the successors of Dr. Siegert.

Amer Picon is a French bitters, or an aperitif, made from French sweet wine infused with bitter herbs.

Orange bitters have a bitter-sweet flavor of the juice of the orange, and is much used in the preparation of cocktails.

There are many bitters which take their names from manufacturers, such as Abbotts, Bookers, Boonekamps, Hostetters, Pychaud, Fernetbranca, etc.

Calisaya is a bitter tonic infused with calisaya or Peruvian bark. It is an aromatic aperitif appetizer, much esteemed in all European cities. It is made in France from the finest quality of muscated wine and Peruvian bark.

VERMOUTH

Italian Vermouth is a bitter-sweet wine. Its component parts are a muscated wine, aromatized with the infusion of herbs and spices and sweetened with pure sugar. It is fortified with brandy to about fourteen to eighteen per cent. Wormwood is one of the chief herbs used in Vermouth, and from it takes its name. It is extensively used in the preparation of cocktails.

French Vermouth is made in and around Cette, France. The French Vermouth differs from the Italian by being less sweet and somewhat lighter in color. In France it is one of the chief aperitifs and makes the finest cocktails and highballs.

BRANDIES OR COGNAC

Brandy is an abbreviation of Brandy Wine, and is a spirituous liqueur obtained by the distillation of wine. The name brandy is also given to the distillates from peaches, apricots, cider, etc. In England a common kind of brandy is distilled from malt liquors, to which the flavor and color of brandy are added, and this is called British brandy.

Cognac brandy is acknowledged the standard, especially those produced in the department of Charente, south of Cognac, France.

California brandies are also much appreciated and are increasing in the estimation of the consumer.

WHISKEY

We may take it as an accepted fact that both by custom and research it has been found that alcohol in its various forms has its legitimate place in the dietary of both healthy and diseased organisms. The uncertainty of its effects, however, compels the medical profession to require a reliable spirit, for unless alcohol is completely eliminated from the organism, its effects, being cumulative, are unsatisfactory; their effects increase in geometrical progression with each succeeding dose. Care must be exercised, therefore, in selecting whiskey or other spirit for general use. Medical opinion seems only to recognize the fact that new whiskey contains oils which are assumed to be amylic alcohol or fusel-oil, and which must be got rid of by rectification or age. Little attention is given to the other essential oils, the secondary products of the more correct materials of distillation. These may be either useful or detrimental in that they assist or retard the elimination of the alcohol.

A properly distilled and well-matured whiskey made from a fully malted barley is the one to be selected. The essential oil of malt being a bland and harmless substance, fulfils a very useful therapeutic office, as by its diaphoretic action upon the skin it promotes and increases excretion, and consequently mitigates the accumulative effects of the alcohol. Both pure malt whiskey as well as genuine cognac brandy possess beneficent qualities in their secondary products, the resulting ethers of which have peculiarly pleasing characteristics.

Amylic alcohol, on the contrary (the essential oil of grain whiskey), is poisonous even in minute doses, and is most difficult to eliminate from the whiskey by any process. Its deleterious effect may be recognized by a paralyzing influence upon the skin, which, closing the doors of escape for the alcohol when consumed, produces feverish symptoms, furred tongue, thirst and headache. Whiskey containing it has earned, therefore, the reputation of being "the Devil in Solution." It is also necessary to avoid spirits of any kind to which saccharine or other softening ingredients have been added. For some reason not apparent in the present state of our knowledge of the chemistry of digestion, the tendency of sugar to turn acid on the stomach is increased when taken in combination with alcohol.

Alcohol plays an important part in the arrest of phthisis —particularly among those who have delicate skins and perspire freely the advantageous effects produced in these cases by the entire abandonment of all medication, and the employment of considerable doses of spirit is well established.

All those cases which are characterized by weakness of the heart, failing circulation, inability to take food, loss of power of sleep, and exhaustion, come under the category of suitable cases in which the best liqueur brandy or fine old malt whiskey is indicated as the most suitable form of alcohol that can be used, no matter how much one has to pay for it.

The physiological action of alcohol of whatever variety is greatly modified by climate, habits of life, and the hourly changes in the atmosphere. A humid climate, whether it be hot or cold, seems not only to tolerate its use, but often to require a stimulant; but in dry and hot countries whiskey should be sparingly used.

RUM

The term rum is an abbreviation of rumbullion. Rum is a spirit, distilled from the juice of sugar cane, and also from molasses, in countries where sugar cane is not cultivated.

The best qualities of rum are made in the West Indies and are named after the place of manufacture, such as Jamaica Rum, Antigura rum, and St. Croix rum.

New England and Medford rum was one of the chief alcoholic drinks of this country, but its consumption has considerably diminished through prohibition laws and the steady advance of the use of whiskey. The medicinal properties of rum are unquestioned, and for home remedies it is still in the lead. As a stimulant it is considered most efficacious. The Medford rums are also made in Massachusetts and enjoy great popularity. They are distilled on the same principle as New England rums.

ALES, BEERS, PORTER, STOUT

Ale is a light colored beer made from malt which is dried at a low heat. (Pale ale is made from the palest or lightest colored malt.)

Beer is the same as the English word ale, and is the common word for all malt liquors. There is, however, a specific distinction. Ale is lighter colored than beer of a certain strength, made from malt and water. Beer is rather darker in color and is made of malt, hops and water.

Stout means a stouter and heavier quality than porter. It is brewed from the high dried malt and is treated in the same way as porter. London and Dublin stouts are considered the best.

Root beer is a beverage containing the extracts of various roots such as dock, dandelion, sarsaparilla and sassafras.

Ginger ale is an effervescent drink very similar to ginger beer. It ranks, however, as an aerated water beverage.

GIN

Gin, a contraction of Geneva, derives its name from the Juniper berry. Originally, it was a national alcoholic beverage in Holland, although Juniper berries do not grow in that country, but always had to be imported from other countries of Europe.

Holland gin, as we know it in this country, tastes and smells strongly of Juniper berries and is known as a very valuable medicine, having a purifying effect on the kidneys if taken in moderation.

The materials used for making the spirit are barley and rye malt and rye. When ground these are mixed with water and some yeast and allowed to ferment. The first result is the production of yeast. The yeast having been taken the fermentation continues for some time; the wash then having the consistency of thin pea-soup is put into the stills, and the first distillation takes place. This distillation is then redistilled when Juniper berries and sometimes hops are added and when distilled again the product is Holland Gin ready for shipment.

Years ago, distillers in Holland gradually started to reduce the quantity of Juniper berries in the distillation of gin for home consumption as a beverage, and as the public seemed to like this, they kept reducing the quantity until at last no Juniper berries were used, though it is sold and consumed in Holland as gin (Jenever).

Only in the best cafés in large cities, do they keep some gin with Juniper flavor. He who wants this has to ask for "Gebeidde Jenever" which means, gin distilled with Juniper berries.

Domestic gins are becoming more popular at the present time than ever before. They are gins distilled in the United States and possess all the attributes of the imported, and in consequence of the heavy import duty, the price is much lower.

My Selection Pickwyck—Dry gin for rickies, fizzes, cocktails, etc.

Gordon and High and Dry are leading imported gins sold in the United States.

The popular taste in England also seems to run to the exclusion of the Juniper flavor, but the English distiller instead of leaving the Juniper berries out, reduces the quantity used and adds a number of other ingredients, the flavor of which almost cover the Juniper flavor.

This English product is known when sweetened as Old Tom Gin, and when unsweetened as Dry Gin and, judging from the increase in consumption in this country, especially of Dry Gin, it seems that the American public likes this combination. It is largely consumed as a beverage in the Gin Fizz, Gin Ricky and various cocktails.

Malt extracts are concentrated, unfermented infusions of malt. They are considered most efficacious in furthering nutrition.

ALCOHOL

Alcohol (ethyl) is the distillate, or product, of anything containing starch or sugar. It is highly inflammable, and burns without smoke or residue. Its normal proof is about 192%.

CELLAR MANAGEMENT

Cellar Temperature.

The most desirable place for the storage of wine is an underground structure. The walls should be thick, with double doors, and the floor dry and concreted. Hot water pipes, skylights or badly fitting doors are most detrimental, as they are destructive to a uniform temperature. There should, however, be an abundance of ventilation, and the thermometer kept at about 56 deg. Fahrenheit, which should not vary more than 2 or 3 degrees upon either the hottest summer or coldest winter day. Excessive heat or cold destroys the life of the wine. A flaming gas jet is not advisable if ventilation is insufficient, because when lighted the temperature rises, creating too much heat near the top of the cellar, and when extinguished it quickly falls.

Binning

There should be only three tiers or bins in the cellar, and the bottles placed in them with their noses inclined, if anything, a little downward, in order to ensure the corks being always kept wet with the wine. The bottles should look as neat and regular as it is possible to make them. Carelessness in binning will, of course, lead to much breakage. Examine each bottle to see that it is properly corked and that there is no leakage before binning away, although, perhaps, an infinitesimal leakage may not be detrimental, but perhaps the reverse. The bottles should not be laid down in the bin unless in good condition, and if not bright must be stood up for twenty-four hours until the deposit has been precipitated, to prevent it settling in the neck of the bottle and coming into the decanter when decanted. Stout young wines of good quality obtain a maturity and generous flavor by being binned in places of moderate warmth, provided, of course, that they are not kept there too long, but champagnes, Rhine wines and Moselles should be kept ir a cool place.

Decanting

Before filling the decanters they should be, of course, thoroughly clean inside and out, and the mouth of the wine bottle very carefully wiped to remove all the exudation which will be found adhering to it; this should ensure the wine being served in perfect condition, for even the slightest cloudiness destroys that delicacy of flavor which is its chief charm. To extract the cork without shaking the wine, the bottle must be taken carefully by the neck with a steady hand and the corkscrew inserted in the exact centre of the cork with the bottle lying in a horizontal position.

Use no strainer, but place a candle in such a position that its light will shine through the wine as it passes between the bottle and the decanter. As soon as any sediment appears, the operation must be stopped at once so that none of it will get into the decanter.

No wine should be served at table that is defective or "corky" (a term to indicate wine that has been tainted by the sap of the cork wood), which is easily detected by the smell.

All wines throw a deposit, rich wines more than others. The crust of Port wine of only one or two years' formation is naturally not so firm as that which has been kept for a longer period. Dry wines take longer to mature than rich.

Port wine should be decanted at the bin in the cellar, from half an hour to two hours before wanted, the decanter being placed in the Dining Room after it is filled, and served at the temperature of the room.

WHEN AND HOW TO SERVE BEVERAGES

Appetizer.—Dry Pale Sherry, plain or with a dash of bitters. Vermouth plain or Cocktails.

With Oysters.—Rhine Wine, Moselle, Dry Sauternes, Chablis or Capri. Cool.

With Soup.—Sherry, Madeira or Marsala. Cool.

With Fish.—Sauternes, Chablis, Rhine Wine, Moselle or Capri, Brolio White. Corvo.

With Entrees.—Claret or Chianti. Temperature of room.

With Roast.—Claret, Burgundy or Chianti. Temperature of room.

With Game.—Champagne (cold); Old Vintage Champagne, cool.

With Game.—Red Burgundy. Temperature of room.

With Pastry.—Madeira, cool.

With Cheese.—Port. Temperature of room.

With Fruit.—Tokay, Malaga or Muscat. Temperature of room.

With Coffee.—Brandy or Cordials. Temperature of room.

If you do not wish to serve such a variety, use the following, viz.:

Either Sherry or Sherry and Bitters, Vermouth or Cocktails as an appetizer.

Either Rhine Wine, Moselle, Sauternes, Chablis or Capri with oysters and fish.

Either Sherry, Madeira or Marsala with Soup.

Either Champagne, Claret, Burgundy, Chianti or Whiskey High Ball throughout the meals.

Either Brandy or Cordials after dinner.

Either Ale or stout with oysters, fish, cold meats, steaks, chops or bread and cheese.

APPENDIX

There is nothing like good advice if only people will take it. An intelligent comprehension of the action of the various alcoholic liquors will do more to advance the cause of temperance than a vigorous adhesion to a dogma. Both Wines and Spirits have undoubtedly their legitimate place in the sustentation of healthy and diseased organism and forms the commonest of all household remedies for a large number of ailments, therefore, the few words upon their dietetic utility will not have been out of place.

As a rule the vigorous frame and perfect digestion of a healthy young or middle-aged person requires only a very moderate allowance, but in failing health and disease the uses of Wines and Spirits are invaluable and numerous. Possibly, however, the differences in their effects are not yet understood, either by the public or even by the majority of medical men, as their action is greatly controlled by their different combinations.

If taken with suitable food and in proper quantities absorption is more gradual, and, being diluted, unquestionably aid the digestion and assimilation of food. Recognizing that these are beverages of ordinary life, their selection must be carefully made, with a due regard to purity as well as to the idosyncrasies of the consumer.

THE GREAT AMERICAN COCKTAIL

Since Dionysius, blithe and young, inspired old Hellaspair
And beat the muses at their game, "with vine leaves in his hair;"
Since Wotan quaffed oblivion to Nieblungen gold,
And Thor beside the icy fjord drank thunderbolts of old;
Since Omar in the Persian bowl forgot the fires of hell
And wondered what the vintners buy so rare as that they sell—
What potion have the gods bestowed to lift the thoughts afar
Like that seductive cocktail they sell across the bar?

Perhaps it's made of whiskey and perhaps it's made of gin;
Perhaps there's orange bitters and a lemon peel within;
Perhaps it's called Martini and perhaps it's called, again,
The name that spread Manhattan's fame among the sons of men;
Perhaps you like it garnished with what thinking men avoid,
The little blushing cherry that is made of celluloid.
But be these matters as they may, a *cher confrère* you are
If you admire the cocktail they pass across the bar.

RECIPES FOR MIXED DRINKS

ABSINTHE.
(American style.)

¾ glass of fine ice
10% of Absinthe
Wine glass of water.
 Shake the ingredients until the outside of shaker is covered with ice.
 Strain in glass and serve.

ABSINTHE COCKTAIL

One dash bitters
90% Absinthe
10% Anisette
Fill glass with fine ice.
 Shake well, until frapped. Strain in cocktail glass and serve.

ABSINTHE DRIPPED

1 pony of Absinthe.
 Fill the bowl of your absinthe glass (which has a hole in the center) with fine ice and the balance with water. Then elevate the bowl and let contents drip into the glass containing the absinthe until the color shows a sufficiency. Pour into a thin bar glass and serve.

ABSINTHE FRAPPE

90% Absinthe
10% Anisette
 Fill glass with fine ice, shake and strain, fill with fizz water and serve.

ALE BEANIE COCKTAIL

50% Irish whiskey
50% Italian Vermouth
Fill glass with broken ice.
 Stir, strain and serve.

ALEXANDER COCKTAIL
(Use bar glass.)

75% rye whiskey
25% Benedictine
1 piece of ice
Twist of orange peel.
  Stir and serve.

AN ALE CUP

Ingredients.—One bottle of Bass Ale, 1 gill of water, 1 glass of Sherry, the juice of two lemons and the fine rind of one, 1 tablespoonful of Castor sugar, a few leaves of fresh mint, a pinch of grated nutmeg, crushed ice.

Method.—Remove the lemon rind well in thin fine strips, put them into a jug, add the sherry, water, lemon juice, sugar, mint and nutmeg, cover and let the liquid stand for 20 minutes, strain into a glass jug, add a few pieces of ice and the ale, then serve.

ALE SANGAREE

Fill up ale glass with ale.
1 teaspoonful powdered sugar.
  Stir gently, grate a little nutmeg on top and serve.

AMER PICON HIGHBALL
(Use large glass.)

One piece of ice in glass.
75% Amer. Picon.
25% grenadine.
  Fill glass with fizz water, stir with spoon and serve.

ANDERSON COCKTAIL
(Use mixing glass.)

75% dry gin.
25% Italian Vermouth.
  Fill glass with cracked ice, twist piece of orange peel, frappe, strain and serve.

ANGOSTURA FIZZ
(Bar glass.)

Tablespoon powdered sugar
Juice half a lemon
Broken ice
½ Pony bitters
White of an egg
Tablespoon of cream
  Shake well with shaker, strain and serve.

ANGOSTURA GINGER ALE

1 glass ginger ale.
3 dashes bitters.

ANGOSTURA GRAPE-FRUIT

Cut the fruit in half, extract the core or pithy substance in the center with a sharp knife, insert the knife around the inner edge of the peel and disengage the fruit from the peel without removing the fruit or breaking the peel, sprinkle plentifully with powdered sugar and dash the opening caused by the removal of the core with Angostura bitters. Ice well before serving.

APOLLINARIS LEMONADE
(Use large glass.)

One tablespoonful of powdered sugar
Three lumps of cracked ice
Juice of one lemon
One pint Apollinaris water.
  Serve with straws.

APPLEJACK COCKTAIL

One dash orange bitters.
100% cider brandy.
½ glass cracked ice, squeeze a piece of lemon peel.
  Stir up with spoon and strain in cocktail glass.
  Drop medium-sized olive in glass and serve.

APPLEJACK SOUR

One teaspoonful of sugar
Juice of one lemon
¾ glass cracked ice
100% cider brandy.
  Stir with spoon, strain in glass, ornament with fruit in season.

APPLE TODDY

1 teaspoonful of sugar dissolved in a little hot water
100% Applejack
¼ of a baked apple
Fill glass ⅔ full of boiling water, stir, grate nutmeg on top, serve.

ARDSLEY COOLER
(Use large thin glass.)

Large piece of ice
Large spray of mint
100% dry gin
1 bottle imported ginger ale.
  Drink with nose to mint.

ARF AND ARF

½ glass porter
½ glass ale.

ASTRINGENT

75% wine glass Port wine
25% glass brandy
3 dashes Angostura bitters
4 or 5 dashes strong Jamaica ginger.
 Stir gently with spoon and serve with a little nutmeg on top.

AUDITORIUM COOLER

Juice of 1 lemon
10 dashes raspberry syrup
1 dash Angostura bitters
1 bottle ginger ale.
 Stir well, ornament with fruit, berries and serve.

AVIATOR

25% Dubonnet
25% French Vermouth
25% Italian Vermouth
25% dry gin
 Fill glass with ice, shake, strain and serve.

BACARDI COCKTAIL

50% Bacardi rum
25% Italian Vermouth
25% French Vermouth
Fill glass with broken ice.
 Stir, strain and serve.

BACHELOR'S ROSE

Juice of a half a lemon
Juice of half lime
Juice of half orange
White of an egg
25% raspberry syrup
75% Sloe gin
Fill glass with cracked ice.
Shake well, strain and serve.

BALTIMORE EGG NOGG

Yolk of an egg
1 tablespoon of sugar
Add a little nutmeg and beat to a cream
50% brandy
25% Madeira wine
3 lumps of cracked ice
25% Jamaica rum.
 Fill glass with milk, shake well, strain into large glass and serve.

BALLOR COCKTAIL

50% Italian Vermouth
50% brandy
½ glass cracked ice.
  Stir, strain and serve.

BAMBO COCKTAIL

50% Sherry wine
50% Italian Vermouth
Dash of orange bitters
½ glass of ice.
  Stir, strain and serve.

BARACCAS COCKTAIL

25% Fernet Branca
75% Italian Vermouth.
  Fill glass with ice, stir, strain and serve.

BARRY COCKTAIL

A very popular drink in 'Frisco.
Place in a small glass a piece of ice
4 dashes bitters
50% Plymouth gin
50% Italian Vermouth
1 piece of twisted lemon peel
5 drops of creme de menthe.
  Stir it well, strain it into a small bar glass and serve with ice water.

BATH COCKTAIL

4 dashes bitters Picon
50% Old Tom gin
50% Italian Vermouth
Fill glass with cracked ice, stir, strain and serve.

B. B. HIGHBALL

Juice of ½ orange
100% Scotch whiskey.
1 piece of ice in glass
Fill glass with ginger ale. Serve.

BEALS COCKTAIL

50% Scotch whiskey
25% French Vermouth
25% Italian Vermouth
½ glass cracked ice.
  Frappe and serve in bar glass.

BEEF TEA.

½ teaspoonful of beef extract
Fill glass with hot water, season with celery salt.
 Stir well and serve.

BENZ COCKTAIL

90% French Vermouth
10% Absinthe
2 dashes Maraschino
 Fill glass with cracked ice, shake, strain and serve.

BICARBONATE OF SODA

1 teaspoonful of bicarbonate of soda
½ glass of water.
 Stir and serve.

BIG FOUR

⅓ Cherry Brandy
⅓ Kirschwasser
⅓ French Vermouth.
 Fill with cracked ice, and shake, strain and serve in cocktail glass.

BIJOU COCKTAIL

(Use large glass.)

¾ glass filled with shaved ice
50% green Chartreuse
40% Italian Vermouth
10% dry gin.
 Stir well with spoon, and after straining in cocktail glass add cherry or small olive, and serve after squeezing lemon juice on top.

BILLIN COCKTAIL

60% Sloe gin
40% Plymouth gin
Fill glass with broken ice
 Stir, strain and serve.

BISHOP

1 teaspoonful of sugar
Juice of ½ lemon
Juice of ½ orange
½ glass of fine ice
Fill glass with Burgundy
Dash of Jamaica rum.
 Stir well, dress with fruits in season, and serve with straws.

BISMARCK COCKTAIL

Two dashes Palmo bitters
One dash Absinthe
100% rye whiskey
Piece of ice in glass
1 slice of orange
  Stir and serve.

BLACK HAWK COCKTAIL

50% rye whiskey
50% Sloe gin
Fill glass with ice.
  Stir, strain and serve in cocktail glass.

BLACKTHORNE COCKTAIL

Fill mixing glass 2-3 full fine ice
1 teaspoonful of syrup
Juice of ¼ lemon
2 dashes orange bitters
50% Italian Vermouth
50% Sloe gin.
  Stir ingredients thoroughly and strain in cocktail glass and serve.

BLACK STRIPE

Use a whiskey glass, with enough Jamaica rum to cover bottom of glass
1 tablespoonful New Orleans molasses.
  Place spoon in glass; hand rum bottle to customer and allow him to stir and help himself.

BLUE BLAZER

(Use 2 metal mugs or 2 heavy bar glasses.)
½ tablespoonful sugar, dissolved in a little water
1 wine glass of Scotch or rye whiskey.
  Set the liquid on fire, and while blazing pour three or four times from one to the other. This will look like a stream of fire; twist a piece of lemon peel on top, with a little grated nutmeg and serve.

BOGERZ COCKTAIL

Juice of half a lime
75% dry gin
25% French Vermouth
Fill glass with broken ice.
  Stir, strain and serve.

BONNETT COCKTAIL

Juice of one lime
50% Benedictine
50% Italian Vermouth
1 piece of ice
1 slice of pineapple.
 Stir, top off with carbonic and serve.

BORNNS' COCKTAIL

1 dash brown Curaçao
50% dry gin
50% Italian Vermouth.
 Stir, strain and serve.

BOSTON COOLER

Peel of lemon in a long string; fill with cracked ice. One bottle of sarsarparilla and serve.

BOTTLE OF COCKTAILS
(For parties.)

1 bottle rye whiskey
1 bottle Italian Vermouth
1 pony glass of Curaçao
1 pony glass of Boker's bitters
Mix well together
Funnel ½ full of fine ice.
 Pass liquor through ice into bottle. Cork well, keep on ice until ready to serve.

BOWL OF EGG NOGG
(For parties.)

1 lb. of sugar
10 eggs. Yolks should be separated. Beat yolks with sugar until dissolved.
Pour in 1 pt. Martell brandy
1 wine-glass of Jamaica rum
3 qts. of rich milk.
 Mix ingredients well with a ladle and stir continually while pouring in milk, to prevent from curdling. Then beat whites of eggs and put on top of mixture. Serve.

BRANDY BURNED WITH PEACH
(Use small bar glass.)

1 wine glass of brandy
½ tablespoon sugar
Burn brandy and sugar together in a saucer.
 Place 2 or 3 slices dried peach in a hot stem glass; pour the burned liquid over it; grate a little nutmeg over it and serve. This is a Southern concoction.

BRANDY CHAMPRELLE
(Use sherry glass.)

25% Curaçao
25% Chartreuse
25% Anisette
25% Kirschwasser or brandy
2 dashes of Angostura bitters.
  Attention should be paid to prevent from mixing.

BRANDY COCKTAIL

1 dash Angostura bitters
100% brandy
½ glass cracked ice.
  Stir, strain and serve.

BRANDY CRUSTA

25% of Maraschino
75% brandy
Juice of one lemon
Fill glass with ice.
  Shake, strain in glass, and trim with fruit in season.

BRANDY DAISY

Juice ½ lemon
Juice ½ orange
Juice ½ lime
10% raspberry syrup
100% brandy.
  One lump of ice. Fill with fizz water and serve.

BRANDY FIX

1 teaspoonful of sugar
Juice of one lime
1 pony pineapple syrup
2 dashes of Chartreuse
Fill glass with cracked ice.
100% brandy.
  Stir with spoon, ornament with grapes and berries in season, serve with straw.

BRANDY FIZZ

1 teaspoonful of sugar
Juice of one lemon
100% brandy
Fill glass with ice.
  Shake well with shaker, strain in glass, fill with seltzer water and serve.

BRANDY FLIP

1 teaspoonful of sugar
1 fresh egg
100% brandy
½ glass cracked ice.

Shake well with shaker, strain and grate a little nutmeg on top and serve.

BRANDY FLOAT.

Fill pony glass with brandy, place whiskey glass over pony of brandy, ½ glass of water, then withdraw pony glass, allowing the brandy to float on top of the water.

BRANDY AND GINGER ALE

1 lump of ice
100% brandy
Bottle of ginger ale
Mix with spoon.

Care should be taken that ale does not foam over the top.

BRANDY HIGH-BALL

1 piece of ice in a glass
100% of brandy.

Fill with fizz water and serve.

BRANDY JULEP

½ teaspoonful of sugar
Add a little water to dissolve sugar
Four sprigs of mint
100% brandy
1 dash of Jamaica rum
Fill glass with ice.

Trim with fruits in season and serve with straws.

BRANDY PUNCH

1 tablespoonful of sugar
A little water to dissolve sugar
25% syrup
100% brandy
½ glass cracked ice.

Shake and strain. Trim with fruit in season. Serve with straws.

BRANDY RICKEY

One piece of ice in glass
Juice of half lime
Drop squeezed lime in glass
100% brandy
Fill glass with fizz water.

Stir with spoon and serve.

BRANDY SANGAREE

1 teaspoonful of sugar
75% brandy
25% Port wine
Fill glass with ice.
  Shake, strain and serve.

BRANDY SCAFFA
(Use sherry glass.)

¼ glass raspberry syrup
¼ glass Maraschino
¼ glass green Chartreuse.
  Top off with brandy and serve like Pousse Café.

BRANDY SMASH

½ teaspoonful of sugar
3 sprigs of fresh mint
100% brandy.
  Fill glass with shaved ice and stir well with spoon, ornament with fruit in season and serve.

BRANDY AND SODA

3 lumps of broken ice
100% brandy
Bottle of plain soda water.
  Stir well with a spoon.
  (This is a delicious summer drink.)

BRANDY SOUR

⅓ teaspoonful of sugar
Juice of ½ lemon
Add a little water to dissolve sugar. Stir well with spoon
  100% brandy
½ glass fine ice.
  Shake, strain in glass and serve with slice of orange.

BRANDY TODDY

  Put in a whiskey glass:
1 teaspoonful of sugar dissolved in a little water
1 small piece of ice.
  Hand the bottle of brandy to the customer and let him help himself.

BRONX COCKTAIL

50% dry gin
25% French Vermouth
25% Italian Vermouth
Twist of orange peel.
  Fill glass with ice, shake and strain, serve.

Classic Cocktail Guides and Retro Bartender Books

BRONX TERRACE

Juice of ½ lime
50% dry gin
50% French Vermouth
Fill glass with ice.
  Shake and strain, serve in cocktail glass.

BROOKLYN COCKTAIL

1 dash Amer. Picon bitters
1 dash Maraschino
50% rye whiskey
50½ Italian Vermouth
Fill glass with ice.
  Stir and strain. Serve.

BRUT COCKTAIL

50% French Vermouth
25% whiskey
25% Calisaya
  Fill glass with cracked ice. Stir, strain and serve.

BUD'S COCKTAIL

1 dash of orange bitters
Twist of orange peel
1 dash of apricot brandy
25% French vermouth
25% Italian vermouth
50% dry gin.
  Fill glass with cracked ice. Shake, strain and serve.

BUTCHER COCKTAIL

50% Scotch whiskey
25% dry gin
25% Italian Vermouth
Fill glass with broken ice.
  Stir, strain and serve.

BYRRH COCKTAIL

25% French Vermouth
25% rye whiskey
50% Byrrh wine
½ glass fine ice
  Stir with spoon until cold. Strain in cocktail glass. Squeeze a piece of orange peel on top and serve.

BYRRH WINE DAISY.

Juice of quarter of an orange
Juice of half a lemon
10% raspberry syrup
90% Byrrh wine
　　Fill glass with broken ice. Shake, strain, fill glass with fizz water.

BYRRH WINE RICKEY

One piece of ice in glass
Juice ½ lime; drop squeezed lime in glass
100% Byrrh wine.
　　Fill glass with fizz water, stir with spoon and serve.

CAFE FOLIES BERGERE

　　To demi-tasse of black coffee add the white of an egg, a pony of Kirschwasser and a pony of brandy. Frappe and serve in small goblet with slice of orange.

CALISAYA COCKTAIL

100% Calisaya
½ glass cracked ice.
　　Stir, strain and serve.

CALIFORNIA SHERRY COBBLER

Large bar glass half full of ice
½ tablespoonful of sugar
1 pony pineapple syrup
1 wine glass California sherry
1 dash bitters.
　　Stir well, fill up with ice, dress with fruit, dash Port wine on top, serve with a straw.

CAMPILL COCKTAIL

1 dash Absinthe
50% rye whiskey
25% French Vermouth
25% Italian Vermouth
　　Fill glass with cracked ice, stir, strain and serve.

CANADIAN FIZZ

½ teaspoon of sugar
100% dry gin
Juice of 1 lime
1 fresh egg
Fill glass with fine ice.
　　Shake well with shaker, strain, top off with fizz water and serve.

CAPTAIN COCKTAIL

50% Brandy
50% Italian Vermouth
Fill glass with cracked ice.
  Stir, strain and serve.

CATAWBA COBBLER

1 teaspoon of sugar
2 wine glasses of Catawba wine
Fill glass with fine ice.
  Dress with fruits in season, and serve with straws.

CHAMPAGNE COBBLER

½ tablespoon of sugar
1 slice of orange
1 piece of lemon peel.
  Fill glass one-third full of fine ice and fill with champagne, dress with fruits in season. Serve with straws.

CHAMPAGNE COCKTAIL

½ lump of sugar
2 dashes of Angostura bitters
½ pint of Ruinart champagne.
  Stir well with spoon, twist a piece of lemon peel on top and serve.

CHAMPAGNE CUP

1 quart champagne
1 pony of brandy
1 pony of Curaçao
1 pony of Maraschino
1 sliced orange
1 sliced lemon
Place large piece of ice in punch bowl.
1 bottle of club soda or syphon.
  Stir well together, add mint and serve.

CHAMPAGNE FRAPPE

  Place the bottle in a Champagne cooler, fill with shaved ice and salt. Turn the bottle for twenty minutes or until the wine becomes almost frozen.

CHAMPAGNE JULEP

1 lamp of sugar
1 sprig of mint
Fill glass with champagne.
  Ornament with fruits in season and serve.

CHAMPAGNE PUNCH
(Use punch bowl.)

4 lumps of sugar
2 ponies of Curaçao
1 quart of Ruinart champagne
Bottle of club soda
Juice of 1 lemon
Stir with ladle
1 large piece of ice.
  Trim with fruits in season.

CHAMPAGNE SOUR

1 lump of sugar
Juice of ½ lemon
Fill glass with champagne.
  Stir well, ornament with fruits in season.

CHAMPAGNE VELVET

For this drink a bottle of champagne and a bottle of porter (both cold) must be used. Fill the goblet half full of porter and balance with champagne, stir with a spoon slowly and carefully and serve.

CHOCOLATE COCKTAIL

Yolk of 1 egg
50% yellow Chartreuse
½ teaspoon of powdered sweet chocolate
Fill glass with cracked ice.
  Shake with shaker, strain and serve.

CHOCOLATE PUNCH

Use large bar glass ⅔ full of fine ice
½ tablespoon sugar
50% port wine
50% Curaçao
1 egg and fill glass with milk.
  Shake thoroughly, strain into a punch glass and grate a little nutmeg on top and serve.

CRIS COCKTAIL

2 dashes Maraschino
50% French Vermouth
50% dry gin
Fill glass with ice.
  Stir, strain and serve.

CHRISTIE COCKTAIL

2 dashes Peychard's bitters
50% dry gin
50% French Vermouth
Fill glass with ice.
 Stir, strain in glass and serve.

CIDER CUP

1 quart cider
1 pony of brandy
1 pony of Curaçao
1 pony of Maraschino
1 sliced orange
1 sliced lemon
1 bottle of Club soda or syphon.
 Place large piece of ice in punch bowl, stir well together, add mint and serve.

CINCINNATI COCKTAIL

½ glass of beer, fill up with soda or ginger ale. This is a palatable drink for warm weather.

CLARENDON COCKTAIL

Mint mulled
Juice of half a lime
100% dry gin
1 bottle Ginger Ale.
 Stir slowly and serve.

CLARET COBBLER

1 teaspoonful of sugar
2 slices of orange
2 slices of lemon
½ glass of cracked ice
Fill glass with claret.
 Stir well with spoon, ornament with fruits in season, serve with straws.

CLARET CUP

1 quart of claret
1 tablespoonful of sugar
1 pony of brandy
1 pony of Curaçao
1 pony of Maraschino
1 pony of Jamaica rum
1 sliced orange
1 sliced lemon
1 bottle of club soda or syphon
Place large piece of ice in punch bowl.
 Stir well together, add mint and serve.

CLARET LEMONADE

2 teaspoonfuls of sugar
Juice of 1 lemon
½ glass cracked ice
¾ glass of water.

Shake well, dress with fruits in season, fill with claret, pour slowly, so it floats on top. Serve with straw.

CLARET PUNCH

1 tablespoonful of sugar
Squirt of seltzer
Juice of ½ lemon
Half glass of cracked ice
Fill glass with claret.

Stir well, and ornament with fruits in season.

CLEAVES DELIGHT

50% Grenadine
50% Italian Vermouth
1 piece of ice in glass.

Stir and serve.

CLIFTIN COCKTAIL

1 dash Angostura bitters
1 dash Curaçao
50% Italian Vermouth
50% rye whiskey
½ glass cracked ice.

Stir, strain and serve.

CLOVER CLUB COCKTAIL

White of 1 egg
Juice ½ lime
Juice ½ lemon
Juice ½ orange
1 tablespoon raspberry syrup
100% dry gin
1 sprig fresh mint

Fill glass with broken ice, shake, strain and serve.

COCKTAIL A LA FUREY

(Use Schoppen glass.)

Fill ½ glass with Carbonic
Use mixing glass
75% Holland gin
10% Italian Vermouth
15% French Vermouth
Fill glass with broken ice.

Shake, strain on top of ½ glass of Carbonic and serve.

CLOVER LEAF

In genuine old-fashioned American hot weather nothing seems to tickle the palate like a good American drink, and the kind selected generally indicates the characteristics of the person drinking. In winter a man will take almost anything that happens to be the fad for the moment, whether highly flavored or not, but in summer the demand is for something that will quench the thirst, whether beer, lemonade or gin rickey or some other beverage. The Clover Leaf is said to be popular in the city of brotherly love. Certainly it is decorative, for it has a soft orchid color, with a rim of white.

Drink is made of:
100% dry gin
10 dashes grenadine
White of an egg
1 sprig of mint

Fill glass with cracked ice, shake well, strain in champagne glass and serve.

COFFEE COCKTAIL

½ teaspoonful of sugar
1 egg
75% port wine
25% Creme De Cocoa
Fill glass with cracked ice.
Shake well, strain and serve.

COFFEE KIRSCH
(Use wine glass.)

½ spoon of sugar
1 pony of Kirschwasser
50% cold black coffee
1 dash of brandy
Fill glass with fine shaved ice.
Frappe and strain in wine-glass and serve.
(After dinner.)

COGNAC A LA RUSSE

1 pony of Cognac
1 slice of lemon
Place on top of glass.
⅛ cut of sugar on top and serve.

COLUMBUS COCKTAIL

60% Italian Vermouth
40% Hostetter's bitters
Fill glass with ice.
Frappe, strain and serve.

CONEY COCKTAIL

50% Italian Vermouth
50% dry gin
½ glass of fine ice.
 Frappe, strain and serve.

CONSOLIDATED COCKTAIL

75% Gordon gin
25% Italian Vermouth
Fill glass with ice.
 Shake well, strain and serve.

COOK COCKTAIL

Juice 1 lemon
75% dry gin
25% Maraschino
White of 1 egg
 Fill glass with broken ice, shake, strain and serve.

CORONATION COCKTAIL

⅓ Orange gin
⅓ Dubonnet
⅓ French Vermouth
Fill glass with broken ice.
 Stir, strain and serve.

COTTON COCKTAIL

1 dash of Absinthe
2 dashes Orange Bitters
Twist of lemon peel
50% Rye whiskey
25% French Vermouth
25% Italian Vermouth
 Fill glass with broken ice, stir, strain and serve.

CREME DE MENTHE ON ICE

Have the cocktail glass filled with fine ice
Fill up with Creme de Menthe
 Serve with straws.

CREME DE MENTHE HIGHBALL

1 piece of ice in glass
100% Creme De Menthe
 Fill glass with fizz water, serve.

CUBAN COCKTAIL

100% Jamaica rum
Juice ½ orange
3 dashes of gum syrup
 Fill glass with cracked ice; stir, strain and serve.

CURACAO PUNCH

Use large bar glass half full of ice
1 tablespoon powdered sugar
3 or 4 dashes lemon juice
50% brandy
30% Curaçao
20% Jamaica Rum
2 dashes bitters
½ glass carbonated water.
  Stir well with spoon, fill up with ice, dress with fruits, serve with straws.

CUSHMAN COCKTAIL

25% French Vermouth
75% dry gin.
Fill glass with ice, shake, strain and serve.

DANIEL WEBSTER PUNCH
(For 12 persons.)

Juice 12 limes
Add granulated sugar sufficient to make paste
1 pt. St. Croix rum
Let it mull for 12 hours
Large block of ice
Add 1 qt. Champagne.

DEAN COCKTAIL

1 dash American Picon
1 dash Maraschino
50% Italian Vermouth
50% rye whiskey
Fill glass with ice.
  Stir, strain in glass and serve.

DEVIL'S COCKTAIL

10% Devil bitters
90% French Vermouth
Fill glass with broken ice.
  Stir, strain and serve.

DOGS' DAYS

100% Scotch whiskey
1 bottle ginger ale.
  2 slices of orange and serve.

DONNELLY'S

1 Cliquot
2 Pommery
3 Ruinart.

DORR COCKTAIL

30% French Vermouth
60% dry gin
10% Italian Vermouth
Twist of orange peel
½ glass fine ice.
  Shake, strain and serve.

DRY MARTINI COCKTAIL

50% dry gin
50% French Vermouth
Fill glass with cracked ice.
  Stir, strain and serve.

DUBONNET COCKTAIL

100% Dubonnet
Fill glass with ice.
  Twist of orange peel, shake, strain and serve.

DUNHAM COOLER

(Use large glass.)

Peel of orange (in one long string). Place in glass
½ glass of fine ice
Juice of 1 orange
100% rye whiskey
1 bottle imported ginger ale.
  Stir slowly and serve.

DUPLEX COCKTAIL

50% whiskey
25% French Vermouth
25% Italian Vermouth
  Strain and serve.

EDNER COCKTAIL

50% St. Raphael
50% dry gin
Twist of orange peel.
  Fill glass with cracked ice, stir, strain and serve in cocktail glass.

EGG LEMONADE

Use large bar glass ⅔ full of fine ice
1 tablespoon powdered sugar
Juice of 1 lemon
1 fresh egg.
  Fill up glass with water, shake thoroughly, strain into a thin lemonade glass and serve.

EGG NOGG, PLAIN

1 tablespoonful of sugar
1 fresh egg
100% whiskey
½ glass of cracked ice.
 Shake well, strain, grate nutmeg on top and serve.

EGG PHOSPHATE

1 teaspoonful of sugar
1 fresh egg
Juice of 1 orange
3 dashes of phosphate
1 glass of cracked ice.
 Shake well with shaker, strain and serve.

EGG SOUR

1 teaspoonful of sugar
Yolk of 1 egg
Juice of ½ lemon
1 dash Curaçao
100% Martell brandy
½ glass cracked ice.
 Shake well with shaker, strain and serve.

ELK'S DELIGHT

Juice of ½ orange
Juice of ½ lemon
100% pure grape juice
1 teaspoonful powdered sugar
1 dash bitters.
 Cracked ice to half fill glass, plain water to finish, shake, serve in 12-ounce lemonade glass. Garnish with slice of orange and cherries.

EVAN'S COCKTAIL

1 dash of apricot brandy
1 dash of Curaçao
1 dash of bitters
100% rye whiskey
Fill glass with cracked ice.
 Stir well, strain and serve.

EVAN'S COOLER

Use large, thin glass
Wine glass of Claret
Bottle of imported ginger ale.
 Serve.

EVANS' SHANDY GAFF
(In glass pitcher.)

1 large piece of ice in pitcher
2 bottles ginger ale
2 glasses of claret.
Dress with fruit in season and serve.

FAIRBANKS COCKTAIL

1 dash Boker's bitters
90% rye whiskey
10% apricot brandy
½ glass of fine ice.
Shake, strain and serve.

FANCY BRANDY, GIN AND WHISKEY COCKTAILS

1 dash of syrup
1 dash of Angostura bitters
1 dash Curaçao
100% brandy
Gin or whiskey
½ glass of fine ice.
Shake and strain, twist a piece of lemon peel and serve.

FANCY CLAIRE
(Use large thin glass.)

100% rye whiskey
2 dashes Amer. picon
1 bottle club soda.
Stir and serve.

FANCY WHISKEY SMASH
(Use a large bar glass half full of ice.)

2 teaspoons sugar
1 wine glass carbonated water
3 sprigs of mint, pressed
1 wine glass whiskey.
Stir well, fill up with ice, trim with fruit and serve.

FARMERS' COCKTAIL

1 dash of Angostura bitters
50% dry gin
30% French Vermouth
20% Italian Vermouth
⅓ glass cracked ice.
Frappe, strain and serve.

FEDORA

1 teaspoonful of sugar, dissolved in a little water
1 slice of lemon
10% brandy
10% Curaçao
60% Bourbon whiskey
20% Jamaica rum.

Fill glass with broken ice, shake well, ornament with fruits in season, serve with straws.

FINE LEMONADE FOR PARTIES

2 lbs. of granulated sugar.

Grate the rind of ten lemons over sugar. Rub in with sugar until the oil is absorbed.

Add 1 gallon of boiling water.

Stir until sugar dissolves, cool, place large piece of ice in bowl, strain through cloth, ornament with fruits in season.

FISH HOUSE PUNCH

⅓ pint lemon juice
¾ pound powdered sugar, dissolved in sufficient water
½ pint brandy
¼ pint peach brandy
¼ pint Jamaica rum
4 tablespoons Angostura bitters
2½ pints cold water.

Ice and serve.

FOLIES BERGERE COOLER

Put a good-sized drink of rum in a large glass with about six strawberries crushed with mint leaves. Add the juice of an orange, the juice of two limes with the limes, other fruit to taste and fill with plain soda. Iced.

FOLIES BERGERE COCKTAIL

Take equal parts of apple jack and dry gin. Add a little lime juice and frappe. Strain and serve.

FOLIES BERGERE POUSSE CAFE

Raspberry syrup, grenadine, maraschino, curaçao, yellow chartreuse and green chartreuse in order named. Serve with a pony of fine champagne, vintage of 1910.

FOWLER COCKTAIL

Juice of half an orange
75% dry gin
20% French Vermouth
5% Italian Vermouth
Fill glass with ice.

Shake, strain and serve.

FRANK HILL COCKTAIL

50% cherry brandy
50% brandy
Twist of lemon peel
½ glass of cracked ice.
 Shake well in shaker, strain into cocktail glass and serve.

FREEMAN'S BLISS
(In glass pitcher.)

1 bottle of Moselle wine
1 pint German seltzer
1 large piece of ice in pitcher.
 Dress with fruits in season and serve.

FRENCH FLAG
(After dinner cordial.)

⅓ grenadine
⅓ Maraschino
⅓ Creme de Yvette.

GIN BUMP
(Use highball glass.)

1 piece of ice in glass
Squeeze half of lime in glass
100% gin
Fill glass with ginger ale.
 Stir and serve.

GIN AND CALAMUS
(Use whiskey glass.)

 Two or three small pieces of calamus root should be placed in a bottle of gin until the essence has been extracted. To serve, hand out glass with the bottle, allow customer to help himself.

GIN AND MILK
(Use whiskey glass.)

 Hand out glass with spoon in and bottle of gin, allow customer to help himself, then fill up glass with cold milk.

GIN COCKTAIL

1 dash bitters
100% dry gin
½ glass cracked ice.
 Stir and strain, twist a piece of lemon peel and serve.

GIN CRUSTA

Peel of ½ lemon in long string
Place in glass
½ glass of fine ice
1 dash of bitters
Juice of ½ lemon
Dash of Maraschino
100% dry gin.
 And serve.

GIN DAISY

Juice ½ lime
Juice ½ lemon
Juice ½ orange
100% dry gin
10% raspberry syrup
Fill glass with fine ice.
 Shake with shaker, strain in glass, fill with siphon and serve.

GIN FIZZ

1 teaspoonful of sugar
Juice of 1 lemon
1 dash cream
100% gin
Fill glass with fine ice.
 Shake, strain, fill glass with fizz water and serve.

GIN FIX

2 teaspoonfuls of sugar
Juice of ½ lemon
Squirt of seltzer
Fill glass with ice
100% dry gin.
 Stir well, ornament with fruits in season and serve.

GIN HIGHBALL

1 piece of ice in glass
100% dry gin.
 Fill glass with fizz water, stir and serve.

GIN JULIP

½ tablespoonful of sugar
3 sprigs of mint
¼ glass of fine ice
100% dry gin.
 Stir well, trim with fruits in season and serve.

GIN AND MOLASSES
(Use whiskey glass.)

Put enough gin in glass to cover the bottom, drop one tablespoon of New Orleans molasses, place spoon in glass, and allow customer to help himself from gin bottle. Use hot water to cleanse glass.

GIN PUNCH
(Use large bar glass half full of ice.)

1 tablespoon raspberry syrup
1 tablespoon powdered sugar, dissolve in seltzer
1 whiskey glass of Holland gin
3 or 4 dashes lemon juice
1 slice of orange
2 dashes maraschino.

Fill up with ice, shake well, dress with pineapple and berries, and serve.

GIN RICKEY

1 piece of ice in glass
Juice of half a lime
Drop squeezed lime in glass
100% of dry gin
Fill glass with fizz water.

Stir with spoon and serve.

GIN SANGAREE

Prepare this drink same as Brandy Sangaree, substituting gin instead of brandy.

GIN SMASH

1 teaspoon of sugar
2 sprigs of mint
Dissolve with little water
100% dry gin
½ glass cracked ice,

Stir well, serve in old fashioned cocktail glass.

GIN SOUR

½ teaspoon of sugar.
100% dry gin
Juice of 1 lemon
½ glass of cracked ice.

Shake, strain, slice of orange and serve.

GIN AND TANSY
(Use whiskey glass.)

This is an old-fashioned and excellent tonic. It is prepared by steeping a bunch of tansy in a bottle of Holland gin, which will extract the essence; when serving, set the glass, with the lump of ice, before the customer, allowing him to help himself.

GIN TODDY
(Use whiskey glass.)

½ teaspoon of sugar, dissolve well in a little water
1 or 2 lumps of broken ice
1 wine glass Holland gin.
  Stir up well and serve.
  The proper way to serve this drink is to dissolve the sugar with a little water, put the spoon and ice into the glass, and hand out the bottle of liquor to the customer to help himself.

GLASGOW FLIP

25% raspberry syrup
1 fresh egg
Juice of 1 lemon
1 lump of ice
Fill glass with ginger ale.
  Stir and serve.

GOLDEN FIZZ

¾ tablespoonful of sugar
Juice of 1 lemon
100% of gin
Yolk of 1 egg
¾ glass of fine shaved ice.
  Shake well in shaker, fill glass with fizz water mix well with spoon and serve.

GOOD LUCK NIGHT CAP

A pony of fine champagne, vintage of 1810, a pony of grenadine, a bottle of plain soda.

GOULD'S RICKEY

Juice of 1 lime
Drop squeezed lime in glass
100% dry gin
6 dashes of raspberry syrup
Fill glass with cracked ice.
  Shake, strain and serve.

GRAHAM COCKTAIL

25% Fernet Branca
75% Italian Vermouth
½ glass of ice.
  Shake, strain and serve in cocktail glass.

GRENADINE HIGHBALL

1 piece of ice in glass
100% grenadine
Fill glass with fizz water, serve.

GUGGENHEIMER COCKTAIL

2 dashes Fernet Branca
100% Italian Vermouth
½ glass cracked ice.
  Shake, strain and serve.

GUM SYRUP

Take 15 pounds loaf or granulated sugar
1 gallon of water.
  Boil for 8 or 10 minutes, then add enough water to make 2 gallons.

HALF AND HALF

  Mix half ale or beer and porter together.
This is the American style.

HAMERSLEY COCKTAIL

¼ of an orange
2 dashes Maraschino
25% Italian Vermouth
75% dry gin.
  Frappe, strain in glass and serve.

HARVARD COCKTAILS
(Use large bar glass.)

2 dashes bitters
2 dashes of orange Curaçao
½ pony Vermouth
½ pony sherry
  Add ice, strain into cocktail glass and serve with twisted lemon peel.

HAMILTON COCKTAIL

75% Dubonnet wine
25% Scotch whiskey
Fill glass with broken ice.
  Stir, strain and serve.

HOCK COBBLER.

  Prepared same as Claret Cobbler, substituting Hock wine instead.

HOCK COBBLER

1 teaspoonful of sugar dissolved in a little water
1 wineglass of Hock wine
  Fill with fine ice, stir and dress with fruits in season, serve with straw.

HOLSTEIN COCKTAIL

1 dash Amer. Picon
50% Cognac
50% blackberry brandy.
 Frappe, strain and serve.

HONOLULU COCKTAIL

½ spoon sugar
Twist of lemon peel
Juice of ½ orange
Juice of ½ lime
1 dash Curaçao
1 dash Angostura bitters
100% gin.
 Fill glass with cracked ice, shake, strain and serve.

HORSES NECK
(Large thin glass.)

2 dashes lemon juice
Peel a lemon in a long string, place in glass, fill glass with ice
1 bottle of ginger ale.
 Serve.

HOT BRANDY SLING

1 teaspoonful of sugar
100% brandy.
 Fill glass with hot water, grate nutmeg on top and serve.

HOT EGG NOGG

1 tablespoonful of sugar
1 fresh egg
100% brandy
Fill glass with hot milk.
 Shake thoroughly with shaker, strain, grate nutmeg on top and serve.

HOT GIN SLING

1 lump of sugar, dissolved in hot water
100% Holland gin
Fill glass with hot water.
 Stir well, grate nutmeg on top, add a slice of lemon.

HOT IRISH PUNCH

2 lumps of sugar
Juice of ½ lemon
Dissolve in a little hot water
100% Irish whiskey
Fill glass with hot water.
 Stir well, place slice of lemon on top, grate nutmeg and serve.

HOT LEMONADE

1 tablespoonful of sugar
Juice of 1 lemon
Fill glass with hot water.
  Stir well and serve.

HOT MILK PUNCH

1 tablespoonful of sugar
50% Jamaica or Medford rum
50% brandy
Fill glass with boiling hot milk.
  Stir well, and grate a little nutmeg on top and serve.

HOT RUM

1 lump of sugar, dissolved in a little hot water
100% Jamaica rum
Fill glass with hot water.
  Stir well, grate a little nutmeg and serve.

HOT SCOTCH

1 lump of sugar
1 dash of bitters
¾ glass boiling water
100% Scotch whiskey.
  Place piece of lemon peel in glass, a few cloves and serve.

HOT SCOTCH TODDY

½ teaspoonful of sugar
Dissolve with a little hot water
100% Scotch whiskey
  Stir, grate a little nutmeg on top and serve.

HOT SCOTCH WHISKEY SLING

½ lump of sugar
¾ glass hot water
1 piece of lemon peel
100% Scotch whiskey
  Grate a little nutmeg and serve.

HOT SPICED RUM

1 lump sugar
½ teaspoonful mixed allspice
Dissolve with a little hot water
100% Jamaica rum
Fill glass with hot water.
  Stir, grate a little nutmeg and serve.

HUDSON COCKTAIL

3 dashes of orange bitters
50% Holland gin
50% French Vermouth
Fill glass with broken ice.
  Stir, strain and serve with olive.

HUNTER COCKTAIL

75% rye whiskey
25% cherry brandy.
  Fill glass with ice, stir, strain and serve.

IDEAL COCKTAIL

1 piece of grape fruit
50% dry gin
25% French Vermouth
25% Italian Vermouth
  Fill glass with cracked ice, shake, strain in cocktail glass and serve.

ILLINOIS THUNDERBOLT.

85% cider brandy or Jersey lightning
15% grenadine
Fill glass with broken ice, stir, strain and serve.

IMPERIAL EGG NOGG.

1 teaspoonful of sugar
1 fresh egg
90% brandy
10% Jamaica rum
  Fill glass with milk. Shake well, strain, grate nutmeg on top, serve.

IMPROVED MANHATTAN COCKTAIL

1 dash bitters
1 dash Maraschino
50% rye whiskey
50% Italian Vermouth
½ glass cracked ice.
  Stir, strain and serve.

IMPROVED MARTINI COCKTAIL

1 dash orange bitters
Dash Maraschino
50% Italian Vermouth
50% dry gin
Fill glass with cracked ice.
  Stir, strain and serve.

IRVING COCKTAIL

50% dry gin
40% French Vermouth
10% Calisaya
Slice of orange
Fill glass with ice.
  Frappe, strain and serve.

ISABELLE COCKTAIL.

50% Creme de Cases
50% grenadine.
  1 lump of ice in glass and serve.

ITALIAN COCKTAIL.

50% Vermouth
25% Fernet Branca
25% grenadine.
  Fill glass with ice. Frappe, strain and serve.

ITALIAN WINE LEMONADE.

2 teaspoonfuls of fine sugar
Little water to dissolve
4 dashes of raspberry syrup
Juice of one lemon
½ glass cracked ice
100% Marsala wine.
  Fill with water, stir and trim with fruits in season. Serve with straws.

JACK KAISER FAVORITE

  To six strawberries and mint leaves, both crushed, add a good drink of Scotch whiskey, mix with plain soda.

JACK RABBIT COCKTAIL.

Juice of ¼ orange
½ tablespoon grenadine
25% dry gin
75% Italian vermouth.
  Fill glass with cracked ice. Shake, strain in cocktail glass and serve.

JACK ROSE

10 dashes raspberry syrup
10 dashes lemon juice
5 dashes orange juice
Juice ½ lime
75% cider brandy.
  Fill glass with cracked ice, shake and strain, fill with fizz water and serve.

JAMAICA RUM SOUR

½ teaspoon powdered sugar
Juice of 1 lemon
100% Jamaica rum.
 Fill glass with ice, shake well, strain and serve.

JAPANESE COCKTAIL

2 dashes Curaçao
50% Italian Vermouth
30% rye whiskey
20% grenadine syrup
 Fill glass with ice, frappe, strain and serve.

JACK ZELLER COCKTAIL

50% orange gin
50% Dubonnet.
 Fill glass with ice, stir, strain and serve.

JENKS COCKTAIL

1 dash Benedictine
50% Italian Vermouth
50% dry gin
 Fill glass with ice, stir, strain and serve with slice of pineapple.

JERSEY COCKTAIL.

1 dash Angostura bitters
50% Italian Vermouth
50% of cider brandy.
 Mix well, twist of lemon peel on top and serve in cocktail glass.

JERSEY LILY POUSSE CAFE
(Use pony glass.)

½ green Chartreuse
½ cognac brandy
10 drops angostura bitters.
 Pour brandy in carefully so it will not mix and serve.

JERSEY SOUR

½ teaspoonful sugar
100% applejack
Juice of 1 lemon
½ glass cracked ice.
 Shake well with shaker, strain top with a little fizz water and serve with slice of lemon.

JERSEY SUNSET

Into a straight champagne glass put a scant teaspoonful of sugar with enough water to dissolve. Add a twist of lemon or lime peel and half a whiskey glass of fine Old Monmouth Applejack. Now put in enough broken ice to cool, fill with water and finish with a dash or two of Angostura bitters, which should not be stirred in, but be allowed to drop slowly through the amber mixture, imparting to it the sunset hues that probably suggested its name.

In winter, instead of ice, hot water is used, making a most genial drink—A Hot Sunset.

JOHN COLLINS
(Use large glass.)

1 tablespoonful of sugar
Juice 1 lemon
Juice ½ lime
3 lumps of ice
100% Holland gin
1 bottle club soda.

Stir up well, remove the ice and serve.

JUDGE SMITH COCKTAIL

90% rye whiskey
10% apricot brandy.

Fill glass with ice, stir, strain and serve.

JUNKINS COCKTAIL.

½ pony orange Curacao.
½ pony maraschino
2 dashes angostura bitters
100% rye whiskey
1 piece of clear ice.

Stir, twist piece lemon peel on top and serve.

JUNE DAISY
(In large glass.)

10 dashes raspberry syrup
Juice ½ lemon
Juice ½ orange
Juice ½ lime
100% dry gin.

Fill glass with fine ice. Shake well together, fill glass with giner ale. Stir with spoon carefully and serve.

JUNE ROSE
(Use large glass for mixing.)

Juice of ½ orange
Juice of ½ lime
Juice of ½ lemon
Teaspoonful raspberry syrup
100% dry gin.

Fill glass with ice. Shake well with shaker, strain, fill glass with fizz water and serve.

KIRSCHWASSER PUNCH

½ teaspoonful sugar
Juice 1 lemon
25% Chartreuse
75% Kirschwasser
Mix well with spoon
½ glass cracked ice.
  Ornament with fruits in season and serve with straws.

KNICKEBEIN

1 dash Angostura bitters
Yolk of 1 egg
½ pony of Benedictine
½ pony of kummel.
  See that different ingredients are not mixed.

KNICKERBOCKER

1 tablespoonful raspberry syrup
Juice 1 lemon
100% St. Croix rum
2 dashes Curaçao
  Fill glass with cracked ice. Trim with fruits in season.

KNICKERBOCKER BAKED.

Break an egg into a sherry glass, add a pony of kummel, then a pony of brandy. Light the brandy and watch the egg cook.

LARCHMONT COCKTAIL

50% Sherry
50% Italian Vermouth.
  Fill glass with cracked ice, stir and serve.

LA ROCHE COCKTAIL

Take equal parts of French Vermouth, Italian Vermouth and dry gin. Add the juice of an orange, frappe and strain.

LAWRENCE COCKTAIL

Three dashes of Paychard Bitters
30% dry gin
20% Italian Vermouth
30% French Vermouth
20% sloe gin.
  Fill glass with broken ice, shake, strain and serve.

LEMONADE
(Use large bar glass, half full of ice.)
1 heaping tablespoonful of sugar
6 or 8 dashes of lemon juice.
Fill up with water, shake well, dress with fruits, serve with straw. When customer wishes lemonade strained, put into smaller glass and place slice of orange in glass.

An Angostura Lemonade is made like the foregoing with the addition of ½ teaspoonful Angostura bitters.

LEONORA COCKTAIL
25% orange juice
50% dry gin
25% raspberry syrup
½ glass cracked ice.
Frappe, strain and serve.

LEOWI COCKTAIL
25% Booth's orange gin
50% dry gin
25% French Vermouth
Fill glass with ice. Stir, strain in cocktail glass and serve.

LIBERAL COCKTAIL
1 dash Amer. Picon
50% Italian Vermouth
50% rye whiskey
Fill glass with cracked ice. Stir and strain, serve.

(After Dinner)
LITTLE MAXINE
(Serve in pony glass.)
⅓ Val. d'Ema (liqueur)
⅓ green Creme De Menthe
⅓ Creme Yvette

LOND TREE COCKTAIL
50% Plymouth gin
25% Italian Vermouth
25% French Vermouth.
Fill glass with ice and shake, strain and serve in cocktail glass.

MAGNUS

1 dash angostura bitters
Juice of ½ orange
Peel of an orange in one string
Place in glass
50% Gordon dry gin
1 bottle imported ginger ale
    Stir and serve.

MAIDEN'S DREAM

¾ pony glass Benedictine or Creme de Cocoa
Fill with heavy cream.
    This drink is admired by ladies.

MAMIE TAYLOR

Peel of lemon in one string, place in glass so it hangs over
100% Scotch whiskey
½ glass with cracked ice.
    Bottle of imported ginger ale and serve.

MANHATTAN COCKTAIL.

1 dash Boker's bitters
50% Italian Vermouth
50% rye whiskey
½ glass cracked ice.
    Stir, strain and serve.

MARY GARDEN COCKTAIL.

75% Byrrh wine
25% French vermouth
1 dash of Curaçao.
    Fill glass with cracked ice; stir, strain and serve.

MARGUERITE COCKTAIL

2 dashes Field's orange bitters
50% Plymouth gin
50% French Vermouth
1 dash absinthe.
    Fill glass with cracked ice. Stir up well with spoon, strain in cocktail glass, drop olive in glass and serve.

MARTINI COCKTAIL

1 dash orange bitters
50% dry gin
50% Italian Vermouth
    Fill glass with ice. Stir, strain and serve.

MAY WINE PUNCH
(Use large punch bowl.)

Two bunches of (Waldmeister) Woodruff cut in two or three lengths. Place it into a large glass, fill up with Martell brandy, cover it up, let it stand for two hours until the essence of the Woodruff is extracted; cover the bottom of the bowl with granulated sugar.
5 bottles club soda over it.
Cut up four oranges in slices
½ pineapple, berries, cherries, grapes
8 bottles Deinhard-Moselle wine
1 bottle Ruinart champagne
50% Curaçao
50% Maraschino
50% brandy.

Then put your Woodruff and brandy, etc., into the three gallons of excellent May wine punch.

Surround the bowl with ice, serve in wineglass in such a manner that each glass will get a piece of all fruits; then fill with ladle and serve.

MEDFORD RUM PUNCH

1 teaspoonful sugar
Juice of ½ lemon
Dissolve in little water
100% Medford rum
½ glass cracked ice.

Stir with spoon, dress with fruits in season and serve with straws.

MEDFORD RUM SMASH

1 teaspoonful sugar
2 sprigs of mint pressed in sugar to extract the essence
100% Medford rum
½ glass cracked ice.

Stir with spoon, dress with fruits in season, serve with straws.

MEDFORD RUM SOUR

1 teaspoonful sugar
Juice of 1 lemon
100% Medford rum.

Fill glass with cracked ice. Stir well with spoon, strain and dress with fruits in season and serve.

MERRY WIDOW

50% Byrrh wine
50% dry gin.

Fill glass with ice. Stir and strain in cocktail glass, twist of orange peel and serve.

METROPOLITAN COCKTAIL

50% French Vermouth
50% brandy
½ glass fine ice.
  Shake, strain and serve.

MILK PUNCH

2 teaspoonsful sugar
1 dash Jamaica rum
100% rye whiskey
2 lumps ice.
  Fill glass with cold milk. Shake and strain, grate little nutmeg, serve with straws.

MILK SHAKE

25% raspberry syrup
2 lumps of ice.
  Fill glass with milk; shake, strain and serve.

MILK AND SELTZER

½ glass seltzer
½ glass milk

MILL LANE COCKTAIL
(Use mixing glass.)

Squeeze and drop ½ lime in glass
1 teaspoonful of grenadine
4 dashes of absinthe
3 dashes Peychand's bitters
100% Bacardi rum.
  Fill glass with cracked ice; shake, strain and serve.

MILLIONAIRE'S COCKTAIL

50% dry gin
40% French vermouth
10% grenadine
Juice of a half lime.
  Fill glass with broken ice, stir, strain and serve.

MINT JULEP
(Large bar glass.)

1 teaspoonful of sugar
Add enough water to dissolve sugar
3 sprays fresh mint, press until extracted
½ glass of ice
100% rye whiskey
  Place four sprigs of fresh mint on top, trim with fruit in season, serve with straws.

MISSISSIPPI PUNCH
(Use large bar glass.)

1 tablespoonful sugar
Enough water to dissolve the sugar
3 or 4 dashes lemon juice
2 dashes angostura bitters
½ wine glass Jamaica rum
½ wine glass Bourbon whiskey
½ wine glass brandy.

Mix well, fill up with ice, trim with fruits, serve with straws.

MONTANA CLUB COCKTAIL
(Use large bar glass, half full of ice.)

2 dashes angostura bitters
2 dashes anisette
50% French vermouth
50% brandy

Stir with spoon; strain in cocktail glass, put in olive and serve.

MONTGOMERY

75% rye whiskey
25% vermouth
1 slice of orange.

Fill glass with ice. Shake, strain and serve.

MORNING COCKTAIL
(Use large glass.)

Fill glass with cracked ice
1 dash Curaçao
1 dash maraschino
1 dash absinthe
1 dash bitters
50% brandy
50% Italian vermouth

Stir with spoon, strain in whiskey glass, twist of lemon peel on top and serve.

MORNING GLORY FIZZ

Juice of 1 lime
Juice of ½ lemon
1 teaspoonful sugar
White of 1 egg
100% Scotch whiskey
½ glass cracked ice.

Shake well with shaker, strain, fill glass with fizz water.

MORNING GLORY

1 teaspoon of sugar
1 teaspoon of raspberry syrup
100% dry gin
Juice of ½ lemon
White of one egg.

Fill glass with cracked ice, shake, strain and serve, add fizz water.

MORTON'S FAVORITE

Crush six strawberries with mint leaves, add a spoonful of sugar, crushed ice, a good-sized drink of brandy, and a bottle of plain soda. Serve in large glass.

MOSELLE CUP

1 quart Moselle
1 pony of brandy
1 pony of Curaçao
1 pony of Maraschino
1 sliced orange
1 sliced lemon
1 bottle of club soda or syphon
Place large piece of ice in punch bowl.
Stir well together, add mint and serve.

"MULLED ALE"

Ingredients.—One quart of Bass & Co.'s Barley Wine, or Strong Ale, one glass of rum or brandy, one tablespoonful of castor sugar, a pinch of ground cloves, a pinch of grated nutmeg, a good pinch of ground ginger.

Method.—Put the ale, sugar, cloves, nutmeg and ginger into an ale-warmer or stew-pan and bring nearly to boiling point, add the brandy and more sugar and flavoring if necessary and serve at once.

MULLED ALE or A BURTON-ON-TRENT.

Take one quart of Bass & Co.'s Barley Wine, or Strong Ale, two eggs, a teaspoonful of powdered ginger or nutmeg, two tablespoonfuls of castor sugar and one ounce of butter. Beat up the eggs separately. Put the ale in saucepan, add the ginger (or nutmeg), sugar and butter. When nicely warm, but not boiling, pour slowly into the jug containing the beaten eggs; stir well and then warm the mixture on fire without bringing to boiling point.

MULLED CLARET

1 lump of sugar
¼ teaspoon cinnamon
¼ teaspoon fine cloves
½ teaspoon fine allspice
3 or 4 dashes of lemon juice
2 dashes bitters
2 jiggers of claret.
 Use a large bar glass, heat a poker red hot and stick into liquid until it boils, strain and serve in hot claret.

MURPHY COCKTAIL

40% Italian Vermouth
40% rye whiskey
20% sloe gin
½ glass cracked ice.
 Frappe and strain. Serve.

NATIONAL GUARD PUNCH

1 tablespoonful sugar
Juice of 1 lemon
Pony or raspberry syrup
100% brandy
Fill glass with cracked ice
2 dashes Jamaica rum.
 Stir well, trim with fruits in season. Serve with straws.

NEW ORLEANS FIZZ

½ teaspoonful of powdered sugar
Juice of half a lime
Juice of half an orange
Juice of half a lemon
Orange flower
White of 1 egg
75% dry gin
1 teaspoonful of cream.
 Fill glass with broken ice, shake for five minutes, strain and serve.

NICHOLAS COCKTAIL

50% orange gin
50% sloe gin
 Fill glass with ice, stir, strain and serve.

NORTH POLE COCKTAIL

75% French vermouth
25% fresh pineapple juice
 Fill glass with broken ice, shake, strain and serve.
 (Dampen edge of glass and dip in powdered sugar.)

OLD DELAWARE FISHING PUNCH

1 tablespoonful sugar
Juice of 1 lemon
Dissolve with a little water
50% St. Croix rum
50% of brandy.

Fill glass with cracked ice; stir well with spoon, dress with fruits in season and serve with straw.

OLD FASHIONED COCKTAILS

1 dash angostura bitters
1 dash Curaçao
Piece of cut loaf sugar
Dissolve in two spoonsful of water
100% liquor as desired
1 piece of ice in glass.

Stir well and twist a piece of lemon peel on top and serve.

OLIVETTE COCKTAIL

(Use large bar glass half full of ice.)

2 dashes syrup
3 dashes orange bitters
3 dashes absinthe
1 dash bitters
100% dry gin

Stir with spoon, strain in cocktail glass, put in olive, twist lemon peel on top and serve.

OJEN COCKTAIL

50% ojen
6 dashes peychand bitters

Fill glass with cracked ice; shake well, strain and serve.

OLD OXFORD COLLEGE MULLED ALE

Take ¼ lb. cinnamon, ¼ lb. cloves, put both into a saucepan with two quarts of water, put it over the fire till it boils, then let it simmer for an hour, then strain it off into a jug, and when cold put the liquid into a bottle and well cork down.

When making mulled ale, add one wineglass of the liquid to every quart of Bass & Co.'s Barley Wine or Strong Ale, adding a little ginger and loaf sugar to taste. Heat the ale over a brisk fire, but be sure not to let it boil, as that alters the flavor, but take it off just before it boils.

Add a few slices of lemon, and a wineglass of gin to every quart.

"ONE YARD OF FLANNEL" or "ALE FLIP"

Put a quart of Bass & Co.'s Barley Wine, or Strong Ale, on the fire to warm, and beat up three or four eggs with four ounces of moist sugar, a teaspoonful of grated nutmeg or ginger and a quarter of good old rum or brandy. When the ale is near to a boil put into one pitcher, and the rum and eggs, etc., into another; turn it from one pitcher till it is smooth as cream.

OPAL COCKTAIL

50% absinthe
50% Italian vermouth
 Shake, strain and serve.

ORANGE COCKTAIL

Juice of ¼ or an orange
1 dash Chartreuse
75% dry gin
25% Italian vermouth.
 Fill glass with broken ice; shake, strain in orange peel and serve.

ORANGEADE

1 spoonful sugar
100% orange juice
25% raspberry syrup
½ glass cracked ice.
 Fill with water or seltzer, trim with fruits in season, serve with straws.

ORCHARD PUNCH

1 tablespoonful orchard syrup
1 tablespoonful pineapple syrup
100% California brandy.
 Fill glass with ice; mix well, trim with fruits in season, 1 dash of port wine and serve with straws.

ORGEAT PUNCH

(Use large bar glass half full of ice.)

50% orgeat syrup
50% brandy
4 or 5 dashes lemon juice.
 Stir well, fill up with ice, dash with port wine, trim with fruit and serve.

OXFORD UNIVERSITY "NIGHTCAP."

Beat up the yolks of eight eggs with refined sugar pulverized and a nutmeg grated; then extract the juice from the rind of a lemon by rubbing loaf sugar upon it, and put the sugar with a piece of cinnamon and a quart of Bass & Co.'s Barley Wine, or Strong Ale, into a saucepan, place it on the fire, and when it boils take it off, then add a single glass of gin, or this may be left out, put the liquor into a spouted jug, and pour it gradually among the yolks of eggs, etc. All must be kept well stirred with a spoon while the liquor is being poured in. If it is not sweet enough add loaf sugar.

OYSTER BAY COCKTAIL

50% Curaçao
50% dry gin
½ glass ice.
Shake, strain and serve.

OYSTER COCKTAIL

(Use star champagne glass.)

½ dozen small oysters
1 dash lemon juice
1 teaspoonful tomato and chile sauce
3 dashes paprika sauce
2 dashes vinegar
1 dash tabasco sauce.
Shake on top a little salt and pepper, stir gently with spoon and serve.

PALMER COCKTAIL

1 dash Amer. Picon
100% rye whiskey
Fill glass with broken ice. Stir, strain and serve.

PALMETTO COCKTAIL

(Mixing glass half full of ice.)

3 dashes angostura bitters
50% Santa Cruz rum
50% Italian vermouth
Stir well, strain into cocktail glass and serve.

PARISIAN

100% Byrrh wine
Juice of 1 lime
2 pieces of ice in glass.
Stir, fill glass with seltzer and serve.

PARISIAN POUSSE CAFE
(Use Pousse Cafe glass.)

2-5 Curaçao
2-5 Kirschwasser
1-5 Chartreuse.
A celebrated drink in Paris.

PARSON'S COCKTAIL

80% high and dry gin
20% Italian vermouth
Piece of orange peel
Fill glass with ice. Frappe, strain and serve in whiskey glass.

PAT COCKTAIL

50% dry gin
40% French vermouth
10% Italian vermouth
1 dash Curaçao
1 dash angostura bitters
1 twist lemon peel
1 piece of ice.
Stir and serve in stein.

PATRICK COCKTAIL

50% dry gin
50% French vermouth
5 drops of green Breton
Fill glass with broken ice. Stir, strain and serve.

PEACH AND HONEY
(Use whiskey glass.)

1 tablespoonful pure honey
100% peach brandy.
Stir with spoon and serve.

PERFECT COCKTAIL

50% dry gin
25% Italian vermouth
25% French vermouth
½ glass of cracked ice.
Stir, strain and serve.

PHEASANT COCKTAIL

50% brandy
50% dry gin
Fill glass with broken ice. Frappe, strain and serve.

PHILADELPHIA BRONX

50% dry gin
40% Italian vermouth
10% French vermouth.

Fill glass with broken ice. Strain into an old-fashioned glass top off with ginger ale and serve.

PHOEBE DELIGHTS

Juice of 4 oranges, 4 lemons and 4 limes.

Strained so as to get all pulp and seeds out, then sugar syrup to sweeten to taste; put same in punch bowl with lots of fine cut ice, then cut one orange, one lime, one lemon and one nice pineapple and one quart of fine Arrack and one quart of good blended rye whiskey and stir all well (and drink freely as a True Elk can't soon get drunk on it, but others better drink sparingly, as it has the goods to do the work, and thank God on September 27th, I will belong to the Order of the Elks and can then do my duty to the "Phoebe Delights") for one person.

(Use large glass)

Fill with fine cracked ice.
Juice ½ lime
Juice ½ orange
Juice ½ lemon
50% arrack
50% rye whiskey.

Stir until well mixed; dress with fruits in season and serve.

PICON COCKTAIL

80% Amer Picon
20% Italian vermouth
½ glass ice

Shake, strain, twist of orange peel and serve.

PLAIN LEMONADE

2 teaspoonfuls sugar
Juice of 1 lemon
½ glass of ice.

Shake well and fill glass with water, strain, trim in fruits of season. Serve with straws.

PONY OF BRANDY

Fill pony glass with best brandy.
Serve with small glass of ice water.

POPE HIGHBALL

1 piece of ice in highball glass
100% Sloe gin.
Fill glass with ginger ale, stir and serve.

PORTER COCKTAIL

10% Italian vermouth
50% French vermouth
40% dry gin
1 spray of fresh mint
Fill glass with ice. Stir, strain and serve.

PORT WINE COBBLER

2 teaspoonsful of sugar
Water to dissolve sugar
100% port wine.
Fill glass with cracked ice. Stir well with spoon, trim with fruits in season and serve with straws.

PORT WINE FLIP

1 teaspoonful sugar
1 egg
100% port wine.
Fill glass with cracked ice. Shake well with shaker, strain, grate a little nutmeg. Serve.

PORT WINE PUNCH

1 tablespoonful of sugar
Juice of 1 lemon
100% port wine.
Fill glass with cracked ice. Stir with spoon, ornament with fruits in season and serve with straws.

PORT WINE SANGAREE

1 teaspoonful of sugar with little water
2 lumps of ice
100% port wine
Stir with spoon, grate a little nutmeg on top and serve.

POSTMASTER

Piece of ice in glass
100% dry gin
Bottle of ginger ale.
Serve.

POUSSE CAFE
(Use liquor pony glass.)

⅙ of raspberry syrup
⅙ of Maraschino
⅙ of green Creme de Menthe
⅙ brown Curaçao
⅙ of yellow Chartreuse
⅙ of Martel brandy.
 Serve.

POUSSE L'AMOUR

¼ glass Maraschino
Yolk of 1 egg
¼ glass vanilla cordial
¼ glass brandy.
 Keep this drink in separate layers and serve.

PREPARING ROCK AND RYE.

1 pt. water
1 lemon cut in quarters
¼ lb. rock candy
½ orange.
 Boil together until rock candy is dissolved; let it cool off; strain through a cloth and add one quart of good rye whiskey.
 Stir well together; ready for use.

PUNCH A LA ROMAINE

1 bottle champagne
1 bottle rum
2 tablespoons angostura bitters
10 lemons
3 sweet oranges
2 pounds powdered sugar
10 fresh eggs.
 For a party of 15.
 Dissolve the sugar in the juice of the lemons and oranges, adding the rind of one orange, strain through a sieve into a bowl, and add by degrees the whites of the eggs, beaten to a froth. Place the bowl on ice till cold, then stir in the rum and wine until thoroughly mixed. Serve in fancy stem glass.

QUEEN'S HIGHBALL

1½ pony Amer. Picon
1 pony grenadine
1 clear piece ice in glass.
 Fill glass with fizz water. Serve.

RANDOLPH

50% dry gin
40% French vermouth
10% Ballor vermouth.

Fill glass with cracked ice shake, strain and serve in bar glass.

RAPHAEL COCKTAIL

50% St. Raphael
40% French vermouth
10% dry gin.

Fill glass with broken ice, stir, strain and serve.

RAYMOND COCKTAIL

Two dashes of Chartreuse
40% dry gin
30% French vermouth
30% Italian vermouth
Twist of lemon peel.

Serve in champagne glass.

RED LION COCKTAIL

50% high and dry gin
40% Italian vermouth
10% Booth's orange gin
½ glass cracked ice.

Stir, strain and serve.

REGENT PUNCH

To one and one-half pints of strong, hot green tea add one and one-half pints of lemon juice, one and one-half pints of Capillaire, one pint Jamaica rum, one pint brandy, one pint Batavia arrack, one pint Curaçao, one bottle champagne, 2 tablespoons Dr. Siegert's genuine Angostura bitters, one sliced pineapple, and two sliced oranges. Mix thoroughly in a punch bowl. Add the wine and ice just before serving.

REMSEN COOLER

(Use a medium size fizz glass.)

Peel a lemon as you would an apple
Place the rind or peeling into the fizz glass
2 or 3 lumps of crystal ice
1 wine-glass of Scotch whiskey
Fill up the balance with club soda or syphon.

Stir up slowly with a spoon and serve.

In this country it is often the case that people call a Remsen cooler where they want Old Tom gin or Sloe gin instead of Scotch whiskey; it is therefore the bartender's duty to mix as desired.

RENAUD'S POUSSE CAFE

⅓ brandy
⅓ Maraschino
⅓ Curaçao.

Put in whiskey glass, mix well with spoon, withdraw spoon and serve. This delightful drink is from a recipe by Renaud of New Orleans.

RHINE WINE COBBLER

(Use large bar glass half full of ice.)

1 tablespoonful of sugar
1 jigger mineral water
2 jiggers Rhine wine.

Fill up with ice, stir well, ornament with fruit and serve with straws.

RHINE WINE AND SELTZER

½ glass seltzer.

Fill with Rhine wine and serve.

RHINE WINE CUP

1 qt. of Rhine wine
1 pony of brandy
1 pony of Curaçao
1 pony of Maraschino
1 sliced orange
1 sliced lemon
1 bottle of club soda or syphon

Place large piece of ice in punch bowl.
Stir well together, add mint and serve.

RICHMOND COCKTAIL

1 dash orange Curaçao
75% French vermouth
25% Italian vermouth

Fill glass with fine ice. Stir, strain and serve.

ROBERT BURNS.

3 dashes of absinthe
50% French vermouth
50% Irish whiskey
½ glass cracked ice.

Stir with spoon, strain and serve.

ROB ROY COCKTAIL.

50% Scotch whiskey
50% Italian vermouth
3 dashes Peychard bitters
½ glass of cracked ice.

Stir, strain and serve.

ROBINSON COCKTAIL

Juice of ½ orange
50% dry gin
40% byrrh wine
½ glass cracked ice.
 Shake, strain and serve.

ROCKY MOUNTAIN COOLER

1 egg
1 teaspoonful of sugar
Juice of 1 lemon
Fill glass with cider
 Grate a little nutmeg on top.
 Serve.

ROGERS ROCK

Drop cherry in glass
10% maraschino
10% orange gin
80% Dubonnet
 Fill glass with cracked ice. Strain and serve.

ROMAN PUNCH

2 teaspoonsful sugar
1 tablespoonful raspberry syrup
Juice of half lemon
Juice of half orange
½ glass cracked ice
2 dashes of Curaçao
100% of brandy
2 dashes of Jamaica rum.
 Stir with spoon, trim with fruits in season. Sprinkle little port wine on and serve.

ROSSINGTON COCKTAIL

50% dry gin
50% French vermouth
Twist of lemon peel.
 Fill glass with broken ice, stir, strain and serve.

ROYAL SMILE

1 tablespoonful of grenadine
50% dry gin
50% applejack
Juice of 1 lemon.
 Fill glass with cracked ice. Strain and serve.

ROYAL SMILE COCKTAIL

Beat up the white of an egg with the juice of an orange. Add a drink of gin, shake well and strain.

ROYAL FIZZ

1 teaspoonful sugar
Juice of one lemon
100% dry gin
1 egg

Fill glass with cracked ice. Shake well, strain, fill with fizz water and serve with straws.

ROYAL PUNCH

1 pint hot green tea
½ pint brandy
½ pint Jamaica rum
100% arrack
100% Curaçao
50% genuine angostura bitters
Juice of 3 limes
1 lemon, sliced
1 cup warm calf's foot jelly
1 cup sugar.

Mix well while heating, and drink as hot as possible. For party of six.

RUBY COCKTAIL

90% dry gin
10% Peychard bitters.

Fill glass with broken ice; shake, strain and serve.

RUM DAISY

1 teaspoonful sugar
1 teaspoonful raspberry syrup
Juice ½ orange
Juice ½ lime
Juice ½ lemon
75% Medford rum

Fill glass with cracked ice. Shake, strain and fill glass with fizz water and serve.

RUM FLIP

Prepare this drink same as gin flip, using Jamaica rum instead of gin.

RUM FLIP
(Western Style.)

½ pint of ale, heated on fire
1 egg beaten up with powdered sugar.

Put the ale in one cup, the egg in another with a small 100% of rum or brandy, pour from one cup into another several times until thoroughly mixed, dash nutmeg on top and serve.

RYE HIGHBALL

1 piece of ice in glass
100% of rye whiskey.
  Fill glass with fizz water and serve.

RYE WHISKEY RICKEY

1 piece of ice in glass
Juice of half a lime
Drop squeezed lime in glass
100% rye whiskey.
  Fill glass with fizz water. Stir with spoon and serve.

SABBATH MORNING CALM

White of one egg
100% dry gin.
  Fill glass with broken ice. Shake, strain and serve.

SAM WARD

Peel ½ lemon in one string
Set into cocktail glass
Fill with fine shaved ice
100% yellow Chartreuse.
  Serve with straws.

SANKEY PUNCH

(For four persons.)

Pony brandy
Pony Benedictine
1 cocktail glass French vermouth
2 cocktail glasses port wine
5 dashes angostura
Yolks of 2 eggs
Tablespoon of sugar.
  Shake well with ice, strain and serve in claret glass.

SARATOGA COCKTAIL

3 dashes pineapple syrup
2 dashes angostura bitters
40% Italian vermouth
50% brandy
10% rye whiskey
  Fill glass with cracked ice. Stir, strain in cocktail glass and serve.

SAUTERNE COBBLER

1 teaspoonful sugar
½ glass cracked ice
Fill glass with sauterne wine.
  Stir with spoon, ornament with fruits in season, and serve with straws.

SAUTERNE CUP

1 qt. of sauterne
1 pony of brandy
1 pony of curaçao
1 pony of maraschino
1 sliced orange
1 sliced lemon
1 bottle of club soda or syphon.
 Place large piece of ice in punch bowl. Stir well together, add mint and serve.

SCHEUER COCKTAIL
(Serve in cocktail glass.)

50% Dubonnet
50% Italian vermouth.
 Cracked ice. Stir and strain. Serve.

SCHULKE COCKTAIL

Juice of one-half lime
50% dry gin
25% orange gin
25% sloe gin.
 Fill glass with broken ice. Stir, strain and serve.

SCOTCH HIGHBALL

1 piece of ice in glass
100% Scotch whiskey.
 Fill glass with fizz water and serve.

SELTZER LEMONADE
(Use large glass.)

2 tablespoonsful of sugar
Juice of 2 lemons
4 or 5 small lumps of broken ice; then fill up the glass with syhpon seltzer.
 Stir up well with a spoon and serve.

SCOTCH WHISKEY RICKEY

1 piece of ice in glass
Juice of ½ lime
Drop squeezed lime in glass
100% Scotch whiskey
 Fill glass with fizz water. Stir and serve.

SHANDY GAFF

Half a glass of lager
Half a glass ginger ale.
 It is also made with half ale, half ginger ale.

SHERRY AND ANGOSTURA

Put 1 dash of bitters in a sherry glass and roll the glass till the bitters entirely covers the inside surface.
Fill the glass with sherry and serve.

SHERRY AND BITTERS

1 dash of bitters.
Fill glass with sherry wine and serve.

SHERRY COBBLER

½ teaspoonful of sugar
100% sherry wine.
Stir with spoon until sugar dissolves. Fill glass with cracked ice. Ornament with mint, and fruits in season, add little port wine on top and straws. Serve.

SHERRY COCKTAIL

¾ glassful of shaved ice
2 or 3 dashes of bitters
1 dash of Maraschino
100% port wine.
Stir up well with spoon, strain into a cocktail glass, put a cherry into it, squeeze a piece of lemon peel on top and serve.

SHERRY AND EGG

1 teaspoonful of sherry
1 fresh egg.
Fill glass with sherry until it floats and serve.

SHERRY FLIP

2 teaspoonsful powdered sugar
100% sherry wine
1 fresh egg
½ glass cracked ice.
Shake well together, strain and serve. Nutmeg if desired.

SHERRY WINE PUNCH

1 teaspoonful sugar
Juice of half lemon
100% sherry wine.
Fill glass with shaved ice. Stir well, trim with fruit and serve with straws.

SHERRY WINE SANGAREE

Prepare this drink same as Port Wine Sangaree, substituting sherry for port.

SHONNARD COCKTAIL

80% Nickolson's gin
15% French vermouth
5% Italian vermouth

Fill glass with broken ice, shake, strain and serve in whiskey glass.

SILVER COCKTAIL

(Use mixing glass half full of ice.)

1 dash gum syrup
2 dashes orange bitters
1 dash angostura bitters
2 dashes Maraschino
50% French vermouth
50% dry gin.

Stir well, strain in cocktail glass, twist lemon peel on top and serve.

SILVER FIZZ

Juice of 1 lemon
1 spoonful sugar
The white of 1 egg
50% dry gin.

Fill glass with cracked ice, shake and strain. Top off with fizz water, and serve.

SILVERMAN

(Use liquor pony glass.)

½ eau-de vie de dantzic
½ mandarinette

SIRLOIN

1 sprig of mint
50% rye whiskey
50% Italian vermouth.

Fill glass with cracked ice, shake, strain and serve.

SLOE GIN BUMP

(Use highball glass.)

1 piece of ice in glass
Squeeze half of lime in glass
100% sloe gin

Fill glass with ginger ale. Stir and serve.

SLOE GIN COCKTAIL

75% sloe gin
25% Italian vermouth.

Fill glass with ice. Stir and strain in cocktail glass. Serve.

SLOE GIN FIZZ
(Use large bar glass.)

Juice of half lemon
100% sloe gin
Half tablespoonful of sugar.
  Fill glass with fine ice, shake, strain, fill glass with fizz water, serve.

SLOE GIN HIGHBALL

One piece of ice in glass
Juice of ½ lime, drop squeezed lime in glass
100% sloe gin.
  Fill glass with fizz water and serve.

SLOE GIN RICKEY

1 piece of ice in glass
Juice of half lime
Drop squeezed lime in glass
100% of sloe gin
  Fill glass with fizz water. Stir with spoon and serve.

SODA COCKTAIL

1 spoonful sugar
3 dashes angostura bitters
Coating inside of glass with sugar, fill quickly with ice, add 1 bottle lemon or plain soda.
  Two slices of orange, stir and serve.

SODA LEMONADE

2 teaspoonsful sugar
Juice of 1 lemon
1 lump of ice
1 bottle of club or lemon soda.
  Ornament with fruits in season and serve with straws.

SODA NEGUS
(Use small punch bowl.)

1 pint of port wine
½ tablespoon angostura bitters
12 lumps loaf sugar
12 cloves
1 teaspoonful nutmeg.
  Put above ingredients into a clean saucepan, warm and stir well; do not let it boil; pour in on this mixture 1 bottle plain soda. Put in punch bowl and serve in cups.

SOUL KISS

½ spoonful sugar
50% Byrrh wine
25% rye whiskey
25% French Vermouth
Juice ½ orange
Fill glass with ice.
  Shake with shaker and strain top off with fizz water.

STARBOARD LIGHT
(Serve in liquor pony glass.)

90% green creme de menthe
10% brandy
  Serve. Delicious after-dinner cordial.

STANTON COCKTAIL

2 dashes Benedictine
50% dry gin
50% French vermouth.
  Fill glass with ice. Stir, strain and serve.

STAR COCKTAIL

1 dash of orange bitters
50% Italian vermouth
50% applejack.
  Fill glass with ice. Stir, strain and serve.

ST. CHARLES PUNCH
(Use large bar glass.)

1 teaspoonful sugar
3 dashes of lemon juice
1 dash seltzer
75% port wine
25% brandy
2 dashes Curaçao
1 dash genuine angostura bitters.
  Stir well, fill glass with shaved ice, trim with fruit and serve with straws.

ST. CROIX CRUSTA
(Use mixing glass half full of ice.)

3 dashes of gum syrup
1 dash of Peychaud bitters
2 dashes of lemon juice
1 dash of mineral water
2 dashes maraschino
100% St. Croix rum.
  Mix well, strain into stem glass, prepared as follows: Remove the peel from one lemon in one long string, put into stem glass after moistening and dipping in sugar.

ST. CROIX FIZZ

1 teaspoonful sugar
Juice of 1 lemon
100% of St. Croix rum
  Fill glass with broken ice. Shake and strain. Fill glass with fizz water and serve.

ST. CROIX RUM PUNCH

1 tablespoonful sugar
Juice 1 lemon
75% St. Croix rum
25% Jamaica rum.
  Fill glass with cracked ice. Stir with spoon, ornament with fruits in season and serve with straws.

ST. CROIX SOUR

½ teaspoonful sugar
Juice of 1 lemon
100% St. Croix rum
  Fill glass with cracked ice. Shake with shaker, strain, trim with fruits in season and serve.

STONE FENCE

100% whiskey
2 lumps of ice.
  Fill glass with cider. Stir well and serve.

STONEWALL

2 lumps of ice
100% brandy
1 bottle of club soda.
  Stir up well with spoon, remove the ice and serve.

STORY COCKTAIL

50% Boonekamp bitters
50% brandy.
  Frappe, strain and serve.

STONY LONESOME

(Use highball glass.)

100% cider brandy
1 slice of orange
1 lump of ice
  Fill with celery tonic; stir and serve.

SWAN COCKTAIL

Juice ½ of one orange
100% absinthe
  Shake, strain and serve.

SWISS ESS

75% white absinthe
25% anisette
White of 1 egg.
 Fill with shaved ice. Shake well in shaker, strain in cocktail glass and serve.

TERMINAL COOLER

Large piece of ice in glass
Peel an orange, in a long string
Juice of ½ orange
100% byrrh wine
2 dashes Curaçao
One bottle ginger ale.
 Serve with straws.

TIP TOP PUNCH
(Use large bar glass with 5 lumps of ice.)
1 dash of lemon juice
1 lump of loaf sugar
2 slices of pineapple
1 slice of orange.
 Fill up with champagne, stir well, dress with berries, dash with genuine angostura bitters, serve with straws.

TOM AND JERRY

Take twelve raw eggs, two liqueur glasses of Creme de Cacao, one bar glassful of Crystal Spring rum, one bar glassful of sherry, one teaspoonful of ground cinnamon, one-quarter of a teaspoonful of ground cloves, and one-quarter of a teaspoonful of ground allspice.

Beat the whites of the eggs to a stiff froth, add the yolks, rum, sherry, cacao and spice. Stir up thoroughly and thicken with fine sugar, until the mixture attains the consistency of light batter. Mix and keep in a cool place.

To serve, take one-half a bar glass of brandy or whiskey, and a dessert spoon of the above mixture. Put in a mug and fill with boiling water or milk, stir slowly, and grate a little nutmeg on top.

TOM AND JERRY
(Use large bowl.)

Take the whites of any number of eggs and beat to a stiff froth.

Add 1½ tablespoonsful of powdered sugar to each egg.

Beat the yolks of the eggs separate.

Stir well together and beat till you have a stiff batter. Add to this as much bicarbonate of soda as will cover a nickel. Stir up frequently, so that eggs will not separate or settle. (To serve.)

Put 1 tablespoonful of batter into Tom and Jerry mug.

100% rum and brandy mixed.

Fill up with boiling water or milk, grate nutmeg on top, stir with spoon and serve.

TOM COLLINS BRANDY
Mix same as above, substituting brandy in place of gin.

TOM COLLINS GIN
1 teaspoonful sugar
Juice of 1 lemon
Juice of ½ lime
2 lumps of ice
100% Old Tom gin
Bottle of club soda.
 Stir with spoon. Serve.

TOM COLLINS RUM
Mix same as above, substituting rum in place of gin.

TOM COLLINS WHISKEY
Mix same as above, substituting whiskey for brandy.

TREASURER COCKTAIL
75% dry gin
25% French vermouth
Twist of orange peel.
 Fill glass with broken ice. Stir, strain and serve.

TRILBY COCKTAIL
(Use mixing glass half full of ice.)

1 dash of orange bitters
1 dash angostura bitters
50% Tom gin
50% Italian vermouth
 Stir well, strain into cocktail glass, add cherry and float creme d'vyette on top.

TROWBRIDGE COCKTAIL
(In whiskey glass.)

1 dash orange bitters
20% Italian vermouth
80% dry gin.
 Twist a piece of orange peel and serve.

TUCKER COCKTAIL
(Use whiskey glass, twist of lemon peel in glass.)

1 dash angostura bitters
25% French vermouth
75% Bourbon whiskey.
 One piece of ice in glass. Stir and serve.

TURF COCKTAIL
(Use mixing glass half full of ice.)

2 dashes absinthe
2 dashes maraschino
2 dashes orange bitters
1 dash bitters
50% Italian vermouth
50% dry gin.

Stir well, strain in cocktail glass, put in olive and serve.

TURF CLUB COCKTAIL

50% Holland gin
50% Italian vermouth.

Strain and serve.

TURKISH SHERBET
(Use a punch bowl.)

Mix as follows:
2 quarts of sweet wine
2 quarts of water
4 pounds of sugar
½ wineglass of angostura bitters
4 lemons, juice only
6 oranges, juice only
1 pound blanched almonds
1 pound muscatel grapes
½ pound figs, cut up
½ pound seedless raisins
1⅓ dozen eggs, whites only
1 dozen cloves, a small piece cinnamon and a little caramel coloring.

Make a hot syrup of the sugar and water and pour it over the raisins, cloves and cinnamon.

When cool, add orange and lemon juice and wine. Strain and freeze in the usual manner.

Take out the spices and add the scalded raisins, figs, grapes and almonds last.

TURN COCKTAIL

4 dashes Boker's bitters
100% sloe gin.

Fill glass with cracked ice, stir, strain and serve.

TUXEDO COCKTAIL
(Use mixing glass half full of ice.)

1 dash maraschino
1 dash of absinthe
3 dashes angostura bitters
50% French vermouth
50% Tom gin

Stir well, strain in cocktail glass, add cherry and serve.

VAN LEE COCKTAIL

50% dry gin
40% Byrrh wine
10% Scotch whiskey.
Fill glass with broken ice. Stir, strain and serve.

VANILLA PUNCH
(Use large bar glass.)

1 teaspoonful of sugar, dissolved in water
2 dashes Curaçao
3 dashes lemon juice
1 dash genuine angostura bitters
25% vanilla cordial
75% cognac brandy.
Stir well, fill up with ice, trim with fruit, serve with straws.

VAN ZANDT COCKTAIL

1 dash apricot brandy
50% French vermouth
50% gin.
Fill glass with ice. Shake, strain and serve.

VELVET CHAMPAGNE
(Use large, thin glass.)

½ pint of champagne
½ pint of stout.
Serve.

VERMOUTH COCKTAIL

1 dash Boker's bitters
100% Italian vermouth
1 dash maraschino.
Fill glass with ice. Frappe, strain and serve.

VERMOUTH FRAPPE

1 dash Boker's bitters
100% Italian vermouth.
Fill glass with ice. Frappe, strain, serve.

VERMOUTH HIGHBALL

1 piece of ice in glass
100% of vermouth.
Fill glass with fizz water, serve.

VICHY

Do not mix in white or red wines as it turns black. It blends well with Scotch and Irish whiskeys.

VIRGIN COCKTAIL
(Use mixing glass half full of ice.)

3 dashes angostura bitters
2 dashes raspberry syrup
50% vermouth
50% Plymouth gin.
 Stir well, strain in cocktail glass and serve.

WASHINGTON COCKTAIL

1 dash angostura bitters
1 dash of Curaçao
90% French vermouth
10% brandy.
 Fill glass with broken ice. Stir, strain and serve.

WATKINS COCKTAIL
(Use mixing glass.)

1 slice of pineapple
1 slice of orange
50% dry gin
25% French vermouth
25% Italian vermouth.
 Fill glass with cracked ice. Shake, strain and serve in bar glass.

WHITE HORSE
(Use large glass)

2 dashes angostura bitters
1 piece of ice
Juice ½ orange
50% Scotch whiskey
1 bottle of ginger ale.
 Stir well with spoon and serve.
 (This is an excellent summer drink.)

WHITE LION
(Use large bar glass, half full of ice.)

1 teaspoonful pulverized sugar
Juice of ½ lime or lemon
100% St. Croix rum
3 dashes Curaçao
3 dashes raspberry.
 Shake well, strain into a stem glass and serve.

WHITE PLUSH

50% rye whiskey
25% maraschino
1 fresh egg.
½ glass cracked ice.
 Fill glass with milk. Shake well with shaker, strain and serve.

WHITE RAT

75% white absinthe
25% anisette.
Fill glass with fine ice. Shake and strain, fill glass with carbonic.

WHISKEY COBBLER

1 teaspoonful sugar
100% whiskey
1 teaspoonful fine apple syrup.
Fill glass with cracked ice. Stir with spoon, dress with fruits in season. Serve with straws.

WHISKEY COCKTAIL

1 dash of angostura bitters
1 dash of orange Curaçao
100% whiskey.
Fill glass with ice. Stir, strain and serve.

WHISKEY CRUSTA

Prepare this drink same as Brandy Crusta, using whiskey for brandy.

WHISKEY DAISY

1 teaspoonful of sugar
Juice ½ orange
Juice ½ lemon
Juice ½ lime
25% raspberry syrup
75% whiskey
Juice of 1 lemon.
Fill glass with cracked ice. Shake, strain, fill glass with fizz water and serve.

WHISKEY JULEP

1 tablespoonful sugar
Squirt of seltzer
3 sprigs fresh mint
Press until essence is extracted
Fill glass with cracked ice
100% of rye whiskey.
Stir well with spoon, dress with fruits in season, sprinkle little sugar on top, dash Jamaica rum. Serve with straws.

WHISKEY FIX

1 teaspoonful sugar
Juice of ½ lemon
100% of rye whiskey.
Fill glass with cracked ice. Stir well with spoon, ornament with fruits in season. Serve with straws.

WHISKEY FIZZ

1 teaspoonful sugar
100% whiskey
Juice of 1 lemon.
 Fill glass with ice. Shake and strain, fill glass with fizz water. Serve.

WHISKEY FLIP

1 teaspoonful sugar
1 egg
Fill glass with cracked ice
100% of rye whiskey.
 Shake, strain and grate a little nutmeg on top and serve.

WHISKEY FLOAT

 Fill glass half full of fizz water. Pour 100% whiskey slowly on top of fizz water and serve.

WHISKEY PUNCH

(Use large bar glass half full of ice.)

1 teaspoonful sugar
4 or 5 dashes lemon juice
100% whiskey and rum mixed
1 dash angostura bitters.
 Shake well, strain into punch glass, with slice of orange, 3 or 4 dashes of Curaçao on top, with seltzer and serve.

WHISKEY RICKEY

1 piece of ice in glass
Juice ½ lime
Drop squeezed lime in glass
100% of Scotch whiskey.
 Fill glass with fizz water. Stir with spoon and serve.

WHISKEY SLING

1 lump of sugar
Enough water to dissolve sugar
2 pieces of ice
 100% of rye whiskey.
 Stir with spoon, grate nutmeg on top and serve.

WHISKEY SMASH

1 teaspoonful sugar
3 sprigs of fresh mint
Little water to dissolve sugar, crush mint until essence is extracted
½ glass cracked ice
100% rye whiskey.
 Stir well with spoon, ornament with fruits in season and serve with straws.

WHISKEY SOUR

½ teaspoon sugar
Juice of 1 lemon
100% rye whiskey.
 Fill glass with ice. Shake well and strain in glass; one slice of orange. Serve.

WHISKEY TODDY

1 teaspoonful sugar
1 teaspoonful water
100% of whiskey.
 Dissolve sugar in a little water, add the whiskey, stir with spoon and serve.

WIDOW'S DREAM
(Use cocktail glass.)

100% benedictine
1 fresh egg.
 Fill up with milk and cream and serve.

WIDOW'S KISS
(Use tumbler.)

Yolk of 1 egg
1 teaspoonful of sugar
100% good rye whiskey.
 Fill glass with cracked ice and shake well together. Fill serving glass half full of seltzer then strain ingredients slowly on top and serve.

WILLIAMS COCKTAIL

Juice of half an orange
75% dry gin
25% Italian vermouth.
 Fill glass with broken ice. Shake, strain and serve.

YORK COCKTAIL

100% Italian vermouth
 Juice of ½ lime in glass, drop peel in glass. Fill glass with cracked ice. Shake, strain and serve.

ZABRISKIE

1 dash Boker's bitters
1 dash maraschino
60% dry gin
40% Italian vermouth
 Fill glass with ice. Stir, strain and serve.

ZAZA COCKTAIL

50% dry gin
50% Dubonnet
Fill glass with ice. Stir with spoon, strain and serve.

ZAZARACK COCKTAIL

(Set old-fashioned glass in ice for three minutes.)
1 dash of absinthe
100% Bourbon whiskey
Quarter loaf of sugar
1 dash of angostura bitters
Piece broken ice in glass.
Stir, strain and serve.

DELICACIES

APPETIZERS

There have been many ways of beginning a meal, those which obtain in our day, outside of oysters and clams when in season, are as a rule made up, in Winter, of caviare, anchovies, tuny, salmon or herring, seasoned highly, served on toast, artichoke bottom, stuffed into small scooped-out tomatoes or apples, or on leaves of lettuce and romain. Fruits such as oranges, grape-fruit or pineapple nicely cooled are also frequently used.

In Summer the fruits above in combination with strawberries, raspberries, cantaloups, and fruit juices are preferred, with reason, for they cool instead of heating the system.

A very good and novel way of starting a lunch, dinner or supper in the hot days for those who cannot use fruit or are tired of canned, smoked or salted fish, is a spoonful of fresh crab meat, nicely seasoned, served in a small glass with two or three small leaves of lettuce, the small glass placed in a large decorated glass filled with ice, thereby keeping the crab meat nice and cold till used.

ANCHOVY SANDWICH

Pour off wine and wash thoroughly in vinegar; then allow them to stand a while in olive oil, after which drain and open lengthwise, removing bones, and place on unbuttered slices of bread.

BISQUIT TORTONI

Put the yolks of four eggs with one and a half tablespoonfuls of sugar, three tablespoonfuls Madeira or sherry wine over the fire, stir till thick; then set aside till cold. Next, when cold, add one pint whipped cream and two ounces powdered sugar with one tablespoonful vanilla. Fill into paper cases, freeze two hours.

CANAPE, WHIMSAY

Make a paste composed half of anchovies and half of tuny fish, season to taste, spread upon a thin square piece of fresh toast, glaze thinly with tartar sauce, decorate the sides with hashed parsley, green pepper, white and yolk of eggs.

CAVIAR SANDWICH

Put caviar on plate, squeezing juice of a fresh lemon on it, with olive oil alternately; beat thoroughly together until paste is formed, and spread on thin toast.

CHEESE STRAWS

One-half pound flour, one-quarter pound butter, one-half pound grated Parmesan cheese, whites of two eggs, little salt and pepper and mustard mixed together; roll very thin and cut in strips one-half inch wide, four inches long; bake light brown.

EGG SANDWICH

Take yolk of hard boiled eggs, adding salt, pepper, mustard and olive oil, making paste, and spread on thin slices of bread.

CHICKEN SANDWICHES

Boil three chickens tender. Remove the bones and put the meat through a chopper, together with three stalks of celery and one small onion, adding the vegetables at intervals during the grinding process. Season with pepper and salt. Pack in a deep dish and pour over it the liquor in which the chicken was cooked. Let stand on ice for several hours. When thoroughly cold, slice thin and lay between layers of bread and butter. If preferred, lamb will serve in place of chicken.

CLUB SANDWICH

Thinly sliced chicken, broiled ham or bacon, with lettuce leaves, on thin slices of buttered toast, seasoned to taste.

LAMB'S KIDNEY SANDWICHES

Split and trim a fresh lamb's kidney. Cut in small pieces, cover with cold water, put over a moderate fire, and heat almost to boiling point, but not quite. Drain off this water, add cold again and repeat the process, doing this three times in all. This method of cooking, the only one which should ever be employed with kidneys for any purpose, leaves them soft and tender. Chop them fine, season well with salt and pepper, mix with melted butter to form a creamy paste, and spread between brown bread slices.

LETTUCE MAYONNAISE SANDWICH

Spread Mayonnaise on thin slices of bread, with leaves of lettuce.

NUT SANDWICH

English walnuts chopped up fine, with mayonnaise dressing, on thin slices of bread.

OLIVE AND WALNUT SANDWICHES

Put English walnuts through the meat chopper, using a rather coarse blade. Drain thoroughly and chop an equal bulk of olives stuffed with pimentos, using a chopping knife and bowl, as the meat chopper squeezes these too dry. Mix, and add enough mayonnaise dressing to make a soft paste. Spread between white or entire wheat bread.

ROQUEFORT CHEESE SANDWICH

Fresh Roquefort cheese, with thick cream, mixed into a paste and spread on thin slices of buttered bread.

SALAD, DON QUIXOTE

Hashed smoked salmon, anchovies, white and yolk of eggs, shallots, chives and beets; seasoned pepper, paprika, oil and vinegar—place a spoonful on a nice leaf of lettuce, add a little fresh caviar on top, serve with a quarter of lemon.

SALMON ON TOAST

Take a nice fresh piece of toast of the desired size, spread over it a slice of canned smoked salmon, trim nicely, sprinkle with bread crumbs and grated Parmesan cheese, add a small piece of fresh butter and brown in a gas salamander.

A tuny fish salad is another which, when made daintily, is both appetizing and satisfying; as also a salad made of cold boiled salmon or sardines wherein radishes, onions, chives, shallots, etc., may be used at discretion. But enough; use your inventive sense and the number becomes unlimited.

THE IMPROVED JACK'S STRAINER

(PATENT APPLIED FOR)

PRICE - - - - - - - - **$1.00**

POST PAID

Classic Cocktail Guides and Retro Bartender Books

Ruinart Brut

Oldest

Champagne

Mark in the World

House Founded in 1729

THE WINE OF THE

Connoisseurs

TO BE HAD AT ALL
HOTELS AND CAFES

ALSO

HAIG & HAIG

Distillers since 1679

Scots Whisky

Sole Agents

ROOSEVELT & SCHUYLER

New York

CELEBRATED PINCH BOTTLE

Historic Cookbooks of the World

GREEN RIVER

THE WHISKEY

WITHOUT A HEADACHE

CESARE CONTI

Sole Agent

Also for ROBBIE BURNS SCOTCH WHISKEY

35 BROADWAY :: :: NEW YORK

Classic Cocktail Guides and Retro Bartender Books

BALLOR VERMOUTH

An Italian Vermouth of Superior Quality

Brilliant, smooth and not too sweet, it is unquestionably the best vermouth for making cocktails and other mixed drinks. The makers, Messrs. Freund, Ballor & Co., of Turin, have been for years purveyors to the Royal House of Italy, and Ballor Vermouth was awarded the Grand Prix at the Turin Exposition, 1911.

Agents for the U. S.

G. S. Nicholas & Co., New York

HIGH & DRY GIN

The Best London Dry Gin

MADE AND BOTTLED IN LONDON BY

BOOTH'S DISTILLERY

ESTABLISHED 1740

Purveyors by Royal Warrant of Appointment to His Majesty King George V. At the Franco-British Exhibition, London, 1908, High & Dry Gin received the Grand Prix, the highest award for Gins.

═

Agents for the U. S.

G. S. Nicholas & Co.

New York

Classic Cocktail Guides and Retro Bartender Books

Marie Brizard & Roger
BORDEAUX

The Leading Cordials of the World

CREME DE MENTHE, APRICOT
BRANDY, CACAO-ANISETTE AND
OTHER SUPERFINE LIQUEURS

Sole Agents for U S.

R. B. HENRY CO., 97 and 99 Hudson St., N. Y.

Classic Cocktail Guides and Retro Bartender Books

SOLE IMPORTERS OF

COBURGER
COBURGER BIERBRAUEREI A. G., COBURG, THUERINGEN

PILSENER
BÜRGERLICHES BRAUHAUS, LEITMERITZ, BOEHMEN

MÜNCHNER KINDL
UNIONS BRAUEREI, SCHUELEIN & CO. MÜNCHEN, BAIERN

R. NAEGELI'S SONS
HOBOKEN, N. J.

Bottle Beer Orders for Hotel, Club and Family Trade Promptly Attended to.

BROLIO

The Standard Chianti Wine

Imported in sealed cases from Baron Ricasoli's Brolio Castle famous cellars in the Chianti district (Tuscany)

Sole Agent for U. S. and Canada

EMILIO PERERA, 11 B'way, New York

Classic Cocktail Guides and Retro Bartender Books

GORDON & CO.
LONDON
Established 1769
ENGLISH DRY GIN

Facsimile of Bottles and Labels

The Gordon Gin Makes a Delicious Cocktail, Fizz and Rickey, also a very refreshing drink with plain soda.

E. LA MONTAGNE'S SONS
SOLE AGENTS

15 South William Street   -   -   -   New York

Historic Cookbooks of the World

F. CHAUVENET

(NUITS, COTE-D'OR),
FRANCE

Burgundy Wines

OF SUPERIOR QUALITY

Romanee *Volnay*
Clos de Vougeot *Pommard*
Chambertin *Beaune*
Nuits *Beaujolais*
Macon

Sparkling Burgundies

"Red Cap."
"Pink Cap," Oeil de Perdrix.

H. P. FINLAY & CO., Ltd.
General Agents
35 SOUTH WILLIAM STREET · NEW YORK, N. Y.

Classic Cocktail Guides and Retro Bartender Books

Gold Seal
Champagne

URBANA WINE CO., Sole Makers, Urbana, N. Y.

AMERICA'S BEST
Equal to the
Choicest Imported Brands

Fermented in the
Bottle by the
French Process

Why Pay Import Duties?

For Sale by all leading Dealers. Served at all First Class Hotels, Restaurants, Cafes, Clubs, etc.

Edward S. McGrath

General Representative

36 Whitehall Street   ::   ::   New York

Classic Cocktail Guides and Retro Bartender Books

BYRRH WINE

THE ORIGINAL AND GREATEST FRENCH APPETIZER

BYRRH WINE

makes a most delicious HIGH BALL

BYRRH WINE is an appetizer par excellence. It can be taken at any time and stimulates the desire for food as no other beverage does It is Agreeable, Pleasant and Beneficial. Among Connoisseurs and Particular People it invariably supplants the Cocktail.

L. VIOLET, Thuir, France

Annual Sale: Ten Million Bottles

BACARDI

Pure Distillation of the Sugar Cane

Manufactured in Santiago de Cuba since 1838

AT BEST CAFES, CLUBS, HOTELS
—AND—
RESTAURANTS

AN INNOVATION

Bacardi Rickey

Bacardi High Ball

NOTHING SUPERIOR

NOTHING QUITE
—SO GOOD—

SOLE AGENT FOR U.S. AND CANADA: D. S. DE JONGH
128 Water Street :: **New York**

Classic Cocktail Guides and Retro Bartender Books

RED ROCK
SPRING WATER
NATURAL AND AERATED
NIPPER BRAND GINGER ALE

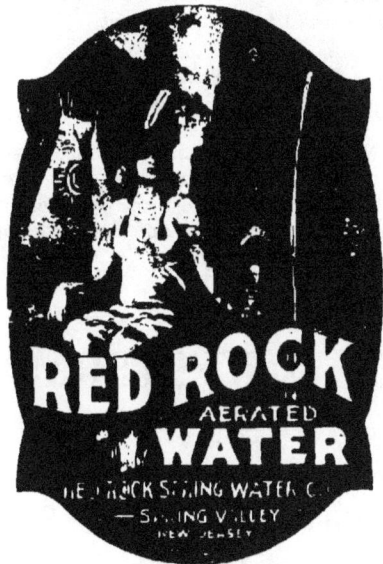

RED ROCK INN
Conducted at the Springs

Spring Valley Road, Bergen County in New Jersey

RED ROCK SPRING WATER CO.
Telephone Connection   **Hackensack, N. J.**

"CRABBIE"
HIGHLAND SCOTCH WHISKY

has impressed the discriminating Consumer as being perfect. It is unsurpassed in delicacy of flavor, of great age and mellowness, and is assuredly second to none in the market for excellence. **Try a case from your Wine Merchant, Grocer or the Distributing Agent.**

F. C. WERNIG
51 STONE STREET, NEW YORK CITY

MR. WERNIG invites the attention of connoisseurs and collectors to the stock of rare old **Sherries, Ports, Madeiras, Brandies,** etc., in his cellars and to his selection of choice **Vintage Château** bottled Clarets and Vintage **Champagnes.**

BUDDE & WESTERMANN
Established 1872

MANUFACTURERS AND IMPORTERS OF

Barroom Glassware, Bottlers' Supplies, Hotel Supplies

ALL UTENSILS FOR THE WHOLESALE AND RETAIL
WINE AND LIQUOR TRADE

TELEPHONE CONNECTION   P. O. BOX 1486

50-52 VESEY STREET, :: NEW YORK
WRITE FOR CATALOGUE OR SALESMAN TO CALL

Classic Cocktail Guides and Retro Bartender Books

THE R. G. McFERRAN CO.
20 SOUTH WILLIAM ST., N. Y.   Telephone 707 Broad

IMPORTERS OF

MITCHELL'S
High Class Scotch and Irish Whiskies

BOUTILLIER G. BRIAND'S
Cognac Brandies

WM. CORRY & CO'S
Belfast Ginger Ale, Etc.

CARLOS MURIAS Y CA.
Key West Havana Cigars

Historic Cookbooks of the World

ALCOHOL 31%

CAMPARI

BITTER

— AND —

CORDIAL

FRATELLI, CAMPARI,

SUCCESSORI

MILANO

SOLE AGENTS FOR THE UNITED STATES

G. G. GRANATA & CO.

IMPORTERS

Stapleton New York (City)

Classic Cocktail Guides and Retro Bartender Books

Classic Cocktail Resource Guide

Some ingredients found in vintage cocktail guides are unavailable or hard to come by today. However, the creation of historically accurate cocktails is a growing hobby and with a bit of Internet research, you will find recipes for bitters and syrups online, as well as manufacturers that are developing new product lines for the classic cocktail enthusiast.

Vendors
A short selection of online vendors selling bitters, mixers, syrups, wine, liqueurs, and spirits. This list is by no means complete but is a good place to start your search.

BevMo!
www.bevmo.com

Binny's Beverage Depot
www.binnys.com

The Bitter Truth
www.the-bitter-truth.com

Cocktail Kingdom
www.cocktailkingdom.com

Fee Brothers
www.feebrothers.com

Hi-Time Wine Cellars
www.hitimewine.net

Internet Wines and Spirits
www.internetwines.com

The Jug Shop
www.thejugshop.com

Monin Gourmet Flavorings
www.moninstore.com

Trader Tiki's Hand-Crafted Exotic Syrups
www.tradertiki.com

The Whiskey Exchange
www.thewhiskyexchange.com

General Interest
These sites provide background information on individual ingredients, suggestions for substitutes, current commercial availability, and recipes.

The Chanticleer Society
A Worldwide Organization of Cocktail Enthusiasts
www.chanticleersociety.org

Drink Boy
Adventures in Cocktails
www.drinkboy.com

The Internet Cocktail Database Ingredients Search
www.cocktaildb.com/ingr_search

Museum of the American Cocktail
www.museumoftheamericancocktail.org

WebTender Wiki
www.wiki.webtender.com

Classic Cocktail Guides and Retro Bartender Books

Coming Soon from
Classic Cocktail Guides
and Retro Bartender Books

Cooling Cups
and Dainty Drinks

A Collection of 19th-Century Cocktails Perfect
for Civil War Reenactments
and Victorian Theme Parties

William Terrington

Illustrations from
"American Dancing Master and Ball-Room Prompter"
by Elias Howe

Now Available from Classic Cocktail Guides
and Retro Bartender Books

Nineteenth-Century Cocktail Creations

How to Mix Drinks: A Bar Keeper's Handbook

George Winter

ISBN: 978-1-880954-30-0

Now Available from Classic Cocktail Guides
and Retro Bartender Books

The Twentieth-Century Guide for Mixing Fancy Drinks

A Pre-Prohibition Cocktail Book

James C. Maloney

ISBN: 978-1-880954-29-4

Now Available from Classic Cocktail Guides
and Retro Bartender Books

The Ideal Bartender

Cocktails and Mixed Drinks
from the Years of the First World War

Tom Bullock
Bartender of the Pendennis Club, Louisville, Kentucky
and of the St. Louis Country Club

Introduction by George H. Walker
Grandfather to President George Herbert Walker Bush
and Great-Grandfather to President George Walker Bush

ISBN: 978-1-880954-31-7

Now Available from Classic Cocktail Guides
and Retro Bartender Books

Daly's Bartender's Encyclopedia

A Pre-Prohibition Cocktail Book

Tim Daly

ISBN: 978-1-880954-32-4

Now Available from Classic Cocktail Guides
and Retro Bartender Books

The Complete Bartender

The Art of Mixing Cocktails, Punches, Egg Noggs, Smashes, Sangarees, Slings, Cobblers, The Fizz, Juleps, Flips, Toddys, Crustas, and All Plain and Fancy Drinks in the Most Approved Style

Albert Barnes

ISBN: 978-1-880954-33-1

Now Available from
Historic Cookbooks of the World

Recipes of the Highlands and Islands of Scotland

A Classic Scottish Cookbook

Compiled by
An Comunn Gaidhealach

ISBN: 978-1-880954-25-6

Now Available from
Historic Cookbooks of the World

Recipes of Sweden

A Classic Swedish Cookbook

Compiled by
Inga Norberg

ISBN: 978-1-880954-27-0

www.ingramcontent.com/pod-product-compliance
Lightning Source LLC
Chambersburg PA
CBHW031448040426
42444CB00007B/1018